Advance Praise for *The 5-minute Gita*

'*The 5-minute Gita* is your new guide to life. It powerfully distils the timeless wisdom of the East for a world with less time.'

Jay Shetty, bestselling author and podcaster

'Nitesh has made a wonderful contribution to modern spiritual books with his *The 5-minute Gita*. It distils the eternal wisdom of the sacred Bhagavad Gita into accessible, bite-sized doses without losing its soul. The writing is intelligent, playful, irreverent when needed, and always anchored in the highest respect for the original. This version may take only five minutes per chapter to read, but its effects, I am sure, will last a lifetime. Do read this book.'

Amish Tripathi, bestselling author and broadcaster

'I remember the first time I read the Bhagavad Gita – the dialogue between Krishna and Arjuna felt as real to me as any conversation I'd had in my own life. When I first glanced through this work, I thought: Is it possible to do justice to the complexity of the Gita with such brevity? But as I read on, it became evident: Nitesh has preserved the voice of Krishna while translating Krishna's message into a language our modern minds – and hearts – can understand and easily apply.'

Gauranga Das, spiritual teacher and author

'In this book, Krishna is the patient, provocative guide we all wish we had. The narrative style allows us to sit beside Arjuna, to eavesdrop on that sacred conversation, and to ask, like Arjuna did: What should I do?'

Devi Chitralekha, spiritual teacher

'What I love about *The 5-minute Gita* is its simplicity and emphasis that spirituality is not an escape – it is engagement.'

Maithili Thakur, singer and
India's cultural ambassador

'Want to understand the Bhagavad Gita but can't find the time? *The 5-minute Gita* makes it easy – no more excuses! In just five minutes a day, over 18 days, you can absorb the wisdom of all 18 chapters. What are you waiting for?! This is *the* spiritual treasure for our times.'

Radhika Das, kirtan artist and Bhakti-yoga teacher

Praise for the *Gita*

'When doubts haunt me, when disappointments stare me in the face, and I see not one ray of hope on the horizon, I turn to *Bhagavad Gita* and find a verse to comfort me; and I immediately begin to smile in the midst of overwhelming sorrow. My life has been full of external tragedies, and if they have not left any visible effect on me, I owe it to the teachings of the *Bhagavad Gita*.'

Mohandas K. Gandhi

'I owed a magnificent day to the Bhagavad-Gita. It was the first of books; it was as if an empire spoke to us, nothing small or unworthy, but large, serene, consistent, the voice of an old intelligence which in another age and climate had pondered and thus disposed of the same questions which exercise us.'

Ralph Waldo Emerson

'In the morning, I bathe my intellect in the stupendous and cosmogonal philosophy of the *Bhagavad Gita*, since whose composition years of the gods have elapsed, and in comparison with which our modern world and its literature seem puny and trivial...'

Henry David Thoreau

'The marvel of the *Bhagavad-Gita* is its truly beautiful revelation of life's wisdom which enables philosophy to blossom into religion.'

Hermann Hesse

'The Bhagavad Gita is the most systematic statement of spiritual evolution of endowing value to mankind. It is one of the clearest and most comprehensive summaries of perennial philosophy ever revealed…'

Aldous Huxley

The 5-minute Gita

The 5-minute Gita
Timeless Wisdom for Everyday Life

Nitesh Gor

BLOOMSBURY
NEW DELHI • LONDON • OXFORD • NEW YORK • SYDNEY

BLOOMSBURY INDIA
Bloomsbury Publishing India Pvt. Ltd
Second Floor, LSC Building No. 4, DDA Complex,
Pocket C – 6 & 7, Vasant Kunj,
New Delhi 110070

BLOOMSBURY, BLOOMSBURY INDIA and the Diana logo are trademarks of Bloomsbury Publishing Plc

First published in India 2025

Copyright © Nitesh Gor, 2025

Nitesh Gor has asserted his moral rights to be identified as the author of this work in accordance with the Indian Copyright Act, 1957

All rights reserved. No part of this publication may be:
i) reproduced or transmitted in any form, electronic or mechanical, including photocopying, recording or by means of any information storage or retrieval system without prior permission in writing from the publishers; or ii) used or reproduced in any way for the training, development or operation of artificial intelligence (AI) technologies, including generative AI technologies.
The rights holders expressly reserve this publication from the text and data mining exception as per Article 4(3) of the Digital Single Market Directive (EU) 2019/790

ISBN: PB: 978-93-69526-91-8; eBook: 978-93-69526-36-9
2 4 6 8 10 9 7 5 3 1

Typeset by Bloomsbury
Printed and bound in India by Thomson Press India Ltd

To find out more about our authors and books, visit
www.bloomsbury.com and sign up for our newsletters

To Pandava Sena – who keep Arjuna's flag flying.
You are the future. And the present.

Contents

Introduction — ix

War Arrives — 1

1. Arjuna's Conflict — 3
2. The Way to Peace — 8
3. The Art of Work — 17
4. Knowledge and Detachment — 24
5. Wisdom in Action — 30
6. Meditation — 36
7. Knowledge and Wisdom — 42
8. Reaching Transcendence — 48
9. The Great Secret — 55
10. The Essence Within — 61
11. Everything, Everywhere, All at Once — 66
12. The Path of Love — 69

13. What's What	74
14. That Which Binds Us	81
15. An Upside-Down Tree	87
16. Good, Bad, and Ugly	91
17. Types of Faiths	95
18. Arjuna Rises	99
Acknowledgements	109
Notes	113
Selected Bibliography	114
About the Author	115

Introduction

The Bhagavad Gita is India's best-known sacred text and it is widely recognised as one of the world's spiritual and philosophical masterpieces – yet it remains one of the world's best-kept secrets. The world knows it and still does not know it. Perhaps this is because people may find it hard to access, particularly if we are familiar only with the concepts of Western philosophy and Abrahamic religions, or if we

Introduction

have only a cursory understanding of concepts such as yoga, karma, and dharma. I certainly felt this when I was fourteen years old which is when I tried to read it for the first time. I managed to get through the whole text only on my third attempt, a few years later. Since then, I have read the text and taught it – to children and adults – many times. It never fails to inspire, and every reading brings with it fresh insights. It is clear to me now why some of the greatest minds through the ages have relied upon it.

The Bhagavad Gita is a battlefield conversation that takes place in under an hour. It features as an episode within the epic Mahabharata, which at 100,000 verses is the world's longest poem and about ten times longer than the Iliad. In only 700 verses, the Bhagavad Gita offers us the wisdom and tools to reframe our perspective at every waking moment and to transform the quality of our relationships with the people around us, our work, the planet, and our very selves. This is no small book. It offers us a new way of thinking about our life, its meaning, and its goal. To become spiritually awake.

My aim in this book is to ease the journey of first-time readers of the Bhagavad Gita. I expect it will take you about five minutes to acquaint yourself with a chapter, and I suggest you read one chapter a day for eighteen days. My hope is that this overview will help new readers quickly grasp the concepts and structure of the text, making it easier to understand and engage with the full version. And for those who are already familiar with the Bhagavad Gita, I hope this book can act as a useful aide-memoire.

Bhagavad-Gita As It Is by A.C. Bhaktivedanta Swami is the best-known translation and commentary on the Bhagavad Gita; it contains the original Sanskrit text in full, Roman transliteration, word-for-word meanings, full prose translation, and commentary. This book will have done its job if it serves as a stepping stone to that great work.

I have relied on translations of the Sanskrit text and commentaries that remain loyal to the origiwnal meaning and have woven them together in my own voice. In doing so, I have tried my best to stay with the original spirit of the work. I want to present the Bhagavad Gita as it was spoken and intended. I ask you, dear reader, to forgive any shortcoming in this regard.

The Bhagavad Gita is not a motivational speech. Nor is it a sermon. It is the voice of a friend who won't let you run from your better self. So open these pages. Let Krishna speak to you. Let Arjuna's questions become your own. And let your journey begin. A great treasure now awaits you!

War Arrives

The year is 3102 BCE. Near what is now New Delhi, India, the battlefield of Kurukshetra stretches endlessly under a vast, fiery sky. The sounds of chariots, elephants, horses, and infantry echo across the plain. Golden armour gleams in the sunlight. The flags of mighty clans flutter violently in the wind. War has arrived.

After the death of the great King Pandu, his half-brother Dhritarashtra was to steward the kingdom until the five virtuous sons of Pandu came of age. But Dhritarashtra and his sons craved the kingdom for themselves, with Dhritarashtra refusing to acknowledge his sons' malevolence and scheming. Pandu's widow, sons and daughter-in-law suffered years of deceit and neglect until finally, after all attempts for peace had been exhausted, they were forced to raise an army to stake their claim to the throne.

On one side was the overwhelming army headed by Dhritarashtra's eldest son, the nefarious Duryodhana, which included the greatest generals of the age. The opposing side was headed by valorous Arjuna, the middle son of Pandu, renowned as the greatest warrior of all. Driving Arjuna's chariot was Krishna, his cousin and friend, whose divinity is revealed through the course of the dialogue. Dhritarashtra was old and blind and so sat in the comfort of his palace in Hastinapura while the armies assembled. His minister Sanjaya narrates in real time what is transpiring on the battlefield.

The scene is now set for an epic fratricidal war – and this is where the Bhagavad Gita begins…

1

Arjuna's Conflict

Dhritarashtra is apprehensive. His army far outnumbers that of the sons of Pandu, but the battlefield is set in a sacred place of pilgrimage, imbued with pious energy that does not bode well for his evil-minded sons. They could lose everything, their lives and the kingdom. He wants to know what is happening on the battlefield. In his veiled opening he asks: is there any hope for my sons? Deep down he knows the answer, but he has become accustomed to ignoring the truth. Are we all not pretty much the same? Contrary to folklore, ostriches don't stick their heads in the sand – but humans do, every time we can't face an uncomfortable truth and wish it away. It might be the morning alarm clock, a toxic relationship, or an impending environmental crisis.

Sanjaya begins by narrating how Duryodhana has just delivered a masterclass in diplomacy to shore up the support of his illustrious generals, many of whom were still sympathetic to the righteous sons of Pandu.

Drums and bugles are sounded for the battle to commence.

Krishna and Arjuna make their appearance – Arjuna as the celebrated warrior and Krishna as the benevolent chariot driver who loves to serve. Arjuna asks Krishna to draw his chariot between the armies: he wants to see all those who have gathered. There is a sense of futility in this request, for what he would see is obvious. This is the first sign of Arjuna's emerging doubt, and Krishna detects it. Krishna draws the chariot in between the armies and his first words are almost playful as he directs Arjuna to behold all those before him.

Seeing the armies thus arrayed, Arjuna is overtaken by compassion and arrives at a pivotal crisis. Though justified by law, how can he fight and kill these people, his friends, teachers, and relatives? Even if he did win, how could he enjoy a kingdom tainted by their blood? Arjuna concludes that anything would be better than the ramifications of this war, even if it means that he and his brothers are cheated out of their kingdom. Even if it means he were to be killed, unarmed and non-combative.

Arjuna is convinced he cannot enjoy fleeting spoils tainted with the blood of his relatives. True enough, but it is not for enjoyment that he should fight. Arjuna wants to walk away, unwilling to be implicated in the evils of killing – but he is ignoring the evils of desertion. His soft-hearted nature urges him to forgive. But he has no right to forgive; his warrior duty to protect society calls on him to fight for justice. Duryodhana is not bound by morality and is therefore not fit to rule. His kingship would debase a flourishing society. It is Arjuna's duty to prevent this. Confused and overwhelmed by grief, Arjuna casts aside his mighty bow and sits down in despair, resolved not to fight.

Arjuna is weighing what he will gain or lose. We all do the same in life, don't we? But in this blinkered way of thinking, we forget the path to peace and happiness, which Krishna will explain as dharma or righteousness. Krishna will teach him, and through him, us, a different way to look at the world.

The root meaning of the word dharma is 'to sustain', and so at its most fundamental level, dharma is 'that which sustains one's existence'. This can refer to the natural harmony at a cosmic, societal, or individual level. Our dharma can be categorised into universal (for example, for all people to strive for truthfulness, self-discipline, compassion, and clarity); personal, according to our roles and functions in society (for example, the householder's dharma to provide for their family, or the teacher's dharma to educate); and spiritual, that is, related to our essential, and eternal, Self. Inevitably, our diverse dharmas come into conflict. For example, one who strives to always be truthful might, say, be doing the wrong thing if their telling the truth would help a murderer find their victim. Krishna will remind Arjuna not to forget his personal dharma as a warrior. He will also deepen this teaching by reminding Arjuna of his spiritual dharma. Our challenge in life is, wherever possible, to find a balance that satisfies these often conflicting dharmas. This is no easy task, but it will be made easier by Krishna's upcoming teachings.

A direct translation of the original Sanskrit title of this first chapter would be 'The Yoga of Despair'. The Bhagavad Gita is the quintessential book of yoga – the art of reconnecting ourselves with transcendence or the art of becoming conscious of a deeper reality. And the Bhagavad Gita jumps right in with this opening chapter, telling us that even despair can be an impetus for yoga. This is a powerful insight: how to use our moments of despair as windows of opportunity for transformation.

Arjuna's dejection will prompt him to recognise that all his physical and mental powers cannot resolve his crisis, leading him to seek spiritual guidance. Einstein understood this quandary when he said that no problem can be solved from the same level of consciousness that created it. Arjuna's compassion is praiseworthy but misplaced; it lacks spiritual knowledge and realisation. He needs help and he is about to realise that. In response, Krishna will propose yoga, the philosophy of the Bhagavad Gita, as the solution.

Arjuna's predicament is also our own. The Bhagavad Gita is Krishna's response to Arjuna…and to us. This philosophy will help Arjuna overcome his fear and grief, and it will help him find peace and harness his own capacity for making mindful choices in seemingly insurmountable circumstances. It can help us in these same ways.

Arjuna's despair has set the scene for the conversation to follow; the next chapter is a concise summary of Krishna's response – ranging from the human condition to the nature of ultimate reality…

2

The Way to Peace

Arjuna knows well the path of self-realisation and has never before shirked his duty, and Krishna urges him not to yield to that weakness now. But Arjuna objects: these so-called enemies are worthy of his respect, particularly his most beloved teachers and elders, regardless of their being compromised by loyalty to a corrupt throne. Inner conflict is tearing him apart; what should he do? What would *you* do? He recognises that he needs help. Desperate, Arjuna asks Krishna to guide him. Sometimes things must get desperate before we will turn for help – but it is never too late. Krishna smiles: now the Bhagavad Gita can begin.

There is a subtle message in Krishna's waiting: he is always there, always available, but he waits patiently, silently, until we invite him to enter our lives. He accepts whatever role we give him and plays it to perfection. So far, Krishna has played the role of Arjuna's friend and charioteer – now he will play the role of his guru. The human condition is perplexing, and we could all benefit from such a guide. Fortunately, the Bhagavad Gita can help fulfil that role for each of us. And Krishna is audible to both sides, indicating the universal nature of his message. Some will listen, some will not – that is our choice.

He begins by telling Arjuna that in all his moral agonising he has been led astray by emotion and he has ignored the basics of spiritual reality. Krishna is not mincing his words. Arjuna's attempt at compassion is materialistic and misapplied, like the attempt to save a drowning person but only managing to rescue their coat. The embodied Self is eternal: it has never not existed nor will it ever cease to be. It is also subatomic in size, yet its influence is felt all over the body – its symptom is consciousness.

Despite our knowledge of biochemical processes, pinpointing the exact change that defines the transition from life to death remains elusive. Science can explain many mechanisms – such as organ failure, cessation of brain activity, or disruption of cellular function – but the precise change that leads to the 'moment' of death is not understood. And it cannot be understood so long as we ignore the role of the Self. Death, simply put, is when the Self leaves the body.

Material nature is ever-changing so the body cannot stay the same even for a moment, whereas spiritual nature is never changing. Therefore, the body cannot be saved, and the Self cannot be killed. The body is constantly changing – though these changes happen imperceptibly. Death is merely another change in the body, where the Self discards the old body and takes on a new one, much like we discard old clothes and put on new ones. Of course, the death of a loved one is painful, but let us not allow this pain to sever us from the reality of what is happening. Those familiar with Plato's Phaedo dialogue will note the similarities, but where Plato's dialogue reaches its climax, the Bhagavad Gita is just getting started!

Unaware of this simple truth, we lose sight of our eternal nature and search for permanence and happiness in all the wrong places. No one wants distress, but it comes anyway. Similarly, happiness also comes. Both come and go, just like the summer and winter seasons. These transient feelings arise from sense perception; we must learn to tolerate them and not be distracted by chasing happiness or dodging distress. Such superficial feelings and sensations are not real in the true sense: something that is real lasts forever; it is indestructible. What is it that cannot be destroyed? Consciousness, the Self. And what is sure to be destroyed? The body. Understanding this difference is the path to liberation. This analytical approach to spiritual knowledge is called sankhya. By becoming fixed on the permanent Self, Arjuna will become steadfast in his duty and remain unaffected by the weakness of heart arising from a fixation on the impermanent body.

Amid cycles of distress and joy, we can remind ourselves: 'This too shall pass.' Now we can expect and prepare for joy *and* distress, endure the winters with resilience and appreciate the summers with detachment, knowing neither will last forever. Meanwhile, we can focus on what we need to do now, for ourselves and for others.

The conversation now takes a slight diversion as Krishna, to leave no room for doubt, proposes that even if Arjuna doesn't believe in an eternal Self, he still has no reason to avoid his duty to fight. Even from a reductive or physicalist point of view, the body, as with all material things, is first unmanifest as atoms, then manifests visibly, and then disintegrates into atoms again. Thus, the brief period of manifestation is not real in any lasting sense. So even if you don't believe in the everlasting Self, why lament over a body that is just a temporary blip?

Krishna also tests Arjuna by tempting him with the incentive of heaven in exchange for fighting a just war and warns him of the infamy he will face for neglecting his duty. Religious scriptures offer such rewards and punishments to lure the materialist towards gradual spiritual elevation, but such trivialities do not move Arjuna. However, like the wider Vedic tradition, the Bhagavad Gita meets us where we are, offering something for everyone – even the most diehard materialist. Any little progress on this journey is valuable, and we must all start somewhere.

Krishna comes back to his main point: rooted in spiritual knowledge, fight for the sake of duty without considering happiness or distress, loss or gain, victory or defeat. We have an obligation to do our duty, dharma, but we do not have a right to the fruits of our actions. It is about doing something for its own sake, not just because we want to do it or because we are chasing results. When we stop trying to avoid our obligatory actions or to enjoy their results, we cease to be implicated in the endless chain of cause and effect, that is, karma, and the consequent cycle of birth and death, that is, samsara. Understanding this helps us put the brakes on karma. This is when we feel lasting relief, peace, and contentment, even in this chaotic world. Such equanimity in the performance of duty is called karma-yoga, and it is the art of work. And when this is combined with deep spiritual knowledge, it is called buddhi-yoga, or the yoga of the intelligence.

A miser does not make good use of their assets, and similarly, those who seek to enjoy the results of their actions, including the material rewards of religious piety, fail to appreciate the true value of their human form. On the other hand, those who have attained enlightenment rise above attraction or aversion to religious formularies, as they are directly in touch with reality.

How can we recognise such a person? Krishna answers: they have no desire for sensory pleasure because their mind is satisfied in their spiritual nature; they are undisturbed by happiness and distress; and they are free from attachment, fear, and anger. Most people are servants of their senses, but an enlightened person controls them, using them when needed and withdrawing them when not, like a tortoise withdrawing its limbs. Become a tortoise! Arjuna must use his mind, body, and senses for the greater good, not for his own satisfaction.

But Arjuna is not so easily convinced: even if we all become 'tortoises' and manage to withdraw our senses, the *desire* for enjoyment remains. And repression doesn't work – the impetuous senses will become active sooner or later. The senses can be like wild horses, dragging the chariot of the mind and body according to their whims, making us feel that we have lost all control. You might recognise this feeling if you have ever tried breaking an old habit. To make change stick, we need anchoring in an alternative that offers something better – something that would naturally tame these unruly horses.

Krishna acknowledges that restraint and philosophical knowledge of the Self are not enough to keep the senses in check. Only better pleasures can help us truly give up lesser ones. Ultimately, this greater pleasure comes from contact with spiritual reality, Brahman.[1] That spiritual reality is accessed in three broad phases: an all-pervading energy, the divinity within each of us, and the transcendent supreme personality. Restraint and knowledge can help us stop focusing on the negative, but we need to redirect our focus to something positive. As the Self comes in touch with these three consecutive phases, it progressively experiences eternity, knowing, and bliss.

Krishna now asserts his divinity for the first time. He clarifies the easiest and most recommended path of yoga: instead of trying to negate the mind and body, use them positively to develop a joyful connection with him. The consequent experiences of eternity, knowing, and bliss provide the greater pleasure that will allow us to genuinely give up the lesser. Now there is no artificial repression and therefore no relapse – instead there is healthy restraint and a positive spiritual experience.

If we don't think about constructive things, we are likely to dwell on the destructive. And if we keep thinking about a particular thing, we become attached to it, and this attachment can become extreme. This invariably leads to anger, either because we don't get what we want or because it lets us down. Then comes delusion, at which point we forget even our own good counsel. This is what it means to 'forget oneself'. This vicious cycle is clearly displayed when we get into frenzied arguments with a loved one. We disregard the importance of the relationship and, ignoring our intelligence, say things we don't really mean and know that we shouldn't.

Without a connection to transcendence, we become victims of our mind as it fluctuates between attraction and aversion, driven solely by what we *think* will bring us happiness and avert distress. We can find no peace in this way of living and thus no happiness. A deep existential fear arises as we become absorbed in an illusory sense of separateness from transcendence. We feel alone and doomed, wholly opposed to our spiritual nature, which yearns for connection and bliss. You can see how this limiting mindset can easily undermine our emotional and mental health.

The path to peace lies in tolerating the incessant flow of desires rather than constantly striving to satisfy them. We can patiently acknowledge our desires without acting on them. When not indulged, and in parallel with our engagement in spiritual practice, the wild horses will gradually calm. Brahma-nirvana is the state of freedom from *selfish* desire. It is not reached by forcing the mind to abolish *all* desires. Without desire, we have no choice and no free will. Desire is an intrinsic characteristic of the Self – for choice to exist, we must have desire. We reach brahma-nirvana, self-realisation, when our desires are aligned with the desires of divinity. Though the Self cannot be free of desire, we can transform the *quality* of our desires through yoga.

Material solutions cannot solve spiritual problems, and if we ignore our spiritual identity, we can expect neither peace nor happiness; the next chapter will explain how we can live a spiritual life in this material world.

3

The Art of Work

Arjuna appears confused. In the previous chapter, Krishna provided some profound spiritual insights to help Arjuna change his perspective and overcome his dilemma. Krishna recommended sankhya (the analytical approach) to distinguish the Self from the body and buddhi (intellect) as the type of yoga he suggested Arjuna practise. These seem, on the surface, like purely intellectual endeavours. But Krishna also told Arjuna to engage in action, dedicating the results of his dutiful work to Krishna. This confuses Arjuna because these methods seem contradictory – one that involves physical activity, and the other two apparently not. Arjuna asks for clarification: does Krishna want him to intellectualise his way through life, or does he want him to act in the world?

The question betrays a common but mistaken assumption that persists even today: that the yoga system comprises discrete paths. Krishna clarifies that physical activity and intellectual pursuit are not opposed. We can integrate different aspects of yoga according to our individual choices and factors such as our level of knowledge or detachment, all of which evolve over time as we advance on our spiritual path.

We can now reconcile Krishna's recommendations in Chapter 2 as follows: buddhi-yoga (also known as bhakti-yoga) is the combination of intellectual analysis (sankhya-yoga, also known as jnana-yoga) and dutiful action (karma-yoga), all lovingly dedicated to divinity. Buddhi/bhakti-yoga = hands + head + heart. It is the most natural path because it accommodates our inclination to act, and it is efficient because, from the outset, it explicitly cultivates the link between the Self and divinity.

Karma-yoga starts by regulating material desires, such as regulating wealth by avoiding unethical means to amass wealth or regulating sex by getting married. At first glance, such types of regulations appear to be restricting our freedom. However, as traffic restrictions lead to an overall increase in driver freedom, these restrictions aim to increase our overall ability to exercise free choice in our lives. And contributing a portion of the fruits of our labours to a good cause is part of karma-yoga to help us develop detachment. Through this combined process of regulation and contribution, we experience a newfound capacity for detachment and free choice. If we are too attached, too driven by habit or addiction, we cannot express free choice. Think of someone who chooses to start smoking – by the time they are on their thousandth cigarette, they are no longer expressing free choice. However, if we are detached and not driven by the demands of our mind and senses, habit or addiction, we find ourselves able to express more free will.

The self-realised person, however, surpasses this stage of dutiful action because their every act is impelled by something greater. Krishna leaves this matter there for now and will explain more in Chapter 5.

Many readers of the Bhagavad Gita are puzzled by why Krishna sometimes uses karma-yoga interchangeably with buddhi/bhakti-yoga. He does this because karma-yoga can be used as an umbrella term for the full spectrum of dutiful action, from dedicating a portion of our labours to some greater cause, all the way to acting out of love for the divine.

It is impossible not to do anything at all, even for a moment. Try it and see! Our minds will quickly get the better of us. We are pleasure-seeking beings, and we are constantly making 'choices' – sometimes good, sometimes bad – to maximise pleasure. And until we reach enlightenment, we act almost helplessly according to our psychophysical nature, even if our intelligence prompts us to do something else. As we learned in the previous chapter, repression will not work. Therefore, rather than risk being a pretender – by artificially stopping worldly activity to pursue spirituality – Krishna recommends that we simply regulate and dovetail our activity with a spiritual purpose.

Even great transcendentalists, who are not obliged to engage in action, continue to perform their duty just to set an example for the rest of us. Whatever a leader does, others will follow, so leaders better lead by example. We are urged to consider what example we would set by walking away from our duty, even when that duty seems unpleasant.

Krishna elaborates that we are often under the illusion that our actions are fully determined by us, unaware that unless we are spiritually awakened, our behaviours are shaped by the conditioning of the gunas or 'modes of material nature'. These modalities, 'goodness', 'passion', and 'ignorance', profoundly influence our minds and actions.[1] When habituated in our ways, we are like rudderless boats being tossed about by the violent waves of our inclinations, desires, and delusions. Our free will is curtailed as we are swept along by our conditioning. How can we expect to make good, mindful choices in such a condition?

A wise person is alert to the difference between materialistic activities and worldly activities that are dovetailed with transcendence. The activity may look the same on the surface, but it boils down to consciousness. Recall the parable of the stonemasons: one is simply 'cutting stones' to earn a living, while the other is 'building a cathedral'. Krishna here repeats his message for Arjuna to dedicate his activities to him, while at the same time cultivating transcendental knowledge. And since each of us has our unique disposition, activities suited for one person may not be suited for another. It is better to do work suited to our own nature even if imperfectly than to try to perform another's work perfectly just because it offers less resistance – imitation, like repression, won't last. In other words, it is not about being perfect, it is about being you.

Arjuna understands and wants to know more. He asks, by what is one impelled to commit negative acts, even unwillingly. Krishna replies that it is lust that impels us to different degrees. Krishna's use of the word kama ('lust'), here and in other parts of the Bhagavad Gita, is not limited to sexual desire; it refers to the range of selfish desires we all harbour – everything from our social media cravings to shopping beyond our means. We all know that feeling. Lust covers the pure consciousness of the Self and, therefore, our rightful experience of eternity, knowing, and bliss. Krishna says that lust is never satisfied and burns like fire. But indulging it is simply adding fuel to the fire or scratching an itch – it will just make things worse. And repressing it is like compressing a spring – sooner or later it will bounce back with a vengeance. So what are we to do?

Krishna concludes by explaining how lust covers the Self. 'Lower' than the Self is the intelligence, then the mind, and then the sensory functions. Lust resides in these functions and thus perverts how we think, feel, and act. The senses are difficult to control, but easier to control than the mind, so we can start there. Regulating our activities will help regulate the fickle mind. Lifestyle rules like waking up early or dietary restrictions are good examples of this. This is why the first two steps of ashtanga-yoga, described in Chapter 6, are the dos and don'ts that aim to regulate our senses and activities. Regulating the senses calms the mind and therefore is essential preparation for the subsequent stages of meditation. Simultaneously, nurturing transcendental knowledge will strengthen our intelligence. A strong intelligence will, in turn, also help to further tame the mind. Ultimately, the most transformative of all will be our spiritual connection with divinity – this will have a powerful trickle-down effect on elevating our intelligence, mind, and senses: lust will be conquered, and we will no longer feel forced to commit negative acts.

The implication is that lust must be transformed into love. Brahma-nirvana was defined in the previous chapter as a stage free from selfish desires. It is the state of self-realisation – the oneness with Brahman. Building on this, we can introduce the positive idea of love, where our desires are transformed and realigned with the desires of divinity. This state of alignment is the complete manifestation of the Self in loving exchange with the source of Brahman. We go from self-realisation to the activity of the self-realised. Love means to desire for and act in the best interests of the beloved. Lust is but a perversion of love: both lust and love involve desire – one is selfish, the other selfless. At its core, yoga is about transforming lust into love.

We all have duties to perform, but the art of work is not to be attached to enjoying their results; this needs knowledge and detachment, which will now be explored further…

4

Knowledge and Detachment

Krishna makes an extraordinary claim: he taught this knowledge of yoga millennia ago. It was then carefully passed down from generation to generation of teachers and disciples to ensure its preservation. Illustrating the importance of relationships in the process of sharing knowledge, Krishna adds that he is repeating his teachings now because Arjuna is so dear to him. When we have something precious or secret

Knowledge and Detachment

to say, we want to know that the person we are sharing it with will treat it with care. A relationship of love is imbued with trust, so sharing hearts is easy. Arjuna asks Krishna how he can possibly claim to have spoken something so long ago! So far Krishna has referred to divinity either in the third person or with only brief reference to himself. Now, to answer Arjuna's question, he will reveal more.

Krishna says that both he and Arjuna have had many lives; Krishna remembers them all, whereas Arjuna does not. This is revealing. During deep sleep we 'forget' our bodies, and an extension of the same forgetfulness occurs when we change bodies at death. The fact that Krishna doesn't forget indicates that he doesn't change his body. He descends to uphold dharma, and he does so by his own sweet will; he is not forced into a material body like we are and is not subject to the cycle of karma. He is the supreme transcendent person – the very form of Brahman. Krishna provides this and further detailed information of his personality and transcendental nature as an important means to stimulate our dormant love for him. Having revived that original love, we will soon attain him – where our love can, at long last, be wholly entrusted and reciprocated.

Knowingly or unknowingly, we are all searching for love – for Krishna, the reservoir and receptacle of love.

He simply reciprocates according to our attitude. Many do not wish to acknowledge him, so they are permitted to continue seeking love in materialism, bound to the cycle of samsara. They choose to remain forgetful. Others may wish to acknowledge only an impersonal phase of transcendence, and they are enabled to do so. Others wish to worship demigods to attain material pleasures. And so on. These different desires reflect varying degrees of conditioning. Krishna remains neutral in all this; he facilitates our desires but does not intervene…unless we want him to. We possess free will as a precondition for love – we cannot love without choice – and Krishna protects our freedom to love him or ignore him. It couldn't be any other way.

Krishna also created a social structure to support our gradual spiritual elevation through dutiful work. This social structure accommodates the varieties of personal qualities and the types of work best suited to our psychophysical natures. The idea is that we can engage our nature so that spiritual pursuit becomes as naturally integrated into our daily lives as possible. In more modern times, this social system has been perverted into a caste system based on birthright. This corruption started a few thousand years ago within ancient India's priestly order, snowballing over time and helped along by centuries of colonisers who misused it as a tool to 'divide and conquer'. But Krishna only speaks of our qualities and our chosen work being social determinants, not of birth. Everyone performs some type of work – this system channels our daily endeavours to become acts of yoga. And society happily benefits as it ticks harmoniously at all levels.

Krishna again explains that action can be inaction and vice versa. If someone acts dutifully and selflessly, they are in effect *not* acting, because such acts do not accrue karma. Consider Arjuna's situation: a soldier who does their duty under proper authority cannot be accused of murder. Similarly, one who fails to act when they should is, in effect, acting through their negligence and thus *will* accrue karma. A deserter may even be sentenced to death. Since we cannot avoid action, let our action be dutiful, detached, and devoted.

This way of acting 'burns up' the karma that would otherwise accrue and bind us to samsara, the cycle of birth and death. Sublimation by this fire of dharma, or dutiful sacrifice, is absolute: it spiritualises everything in its path, including the individual, the act, any intermediary, and so on. For example, a person working in an ordinary office can, by sincerely dedicating the results of their labours to transcendence, gradually elevate themselves, their colleagues, and their workplace. They can do this very simply and very practically: by their ethical behaviour, by donating some of their salary, by reminding themselves of the underlying spiritual essence of all the people around them, by helping their organisation recognise the importance of spiritual well-being, and so on.

People will perform different types of 'sacrifices' according to their social context. Students can use their intellect and attention, householders can use their resources, and retirees can dedicate their time for others. Even mystics dedicate their breath and austerities to a greater purpose. And as with the earlier stages of karma-yoga, they will all make progress, even if their sacrifice is not entirely selfless. Sacrifice can be physical, intellectual, or emotional; that is up to us. The specific form it takes will depend on our consciousness, knowledge, and faith – why we are doing something, with what understanding, and where we are reposing our affections. This is what differentiates the different stages of yoga.

No one can be happy in this world without some form of effort or sacrifice, so it is best we engage in it appropriately. As we know, staying fit is hard, but being unhealthy is harder. Properly done, sacrifice not only frees us from karmic reactions but also awards self-control and detachment, culminating in knowledge as we gradually perceive and experience deeper dimensions of reality. And in this world, there is nothing as pure as knowledge. This knowledge further perfects our detachment from the world.

Krishna's advice is to approach a spiritual master to understand this, for those who have seen the truth can reveal it to us. In Chapter 2, Arjuna asked Krishna how to recognise an enlightened person. Krishna provided a brief reply; Arjuna will pursue the question again in Chapter 14. Anyone and everyone can benefit from the liberating effects of transcendental knowledge. On the other hand, those who choose to remain in ignorance continue in the cycle of birth and death for as long as they desire.

Convinced by this, Arjuna must slash his misgivings with the sword of knowledge and, armed with yoga, perform his duty.

Working with spiritual intention and detachment frees us from material bonds; Krishna will now combine this with the counterintuitive idea from Chapter 3, that we should perform our duties without attachment to their results, into a single formula for everyday spirituality…

5

Wisdom in Action

Arjuna has been paying close attention and wants to leave no stone unturned. In Chapter 3, Krishna said that self-realised persons, illumined by knowledge, have no duty to perform. Arjuna understands from this that the path of knowledge involves giving up working in the world. Yet, Krishna has also emphasised work dedicated to him. Work and renunciation still seem incompatible: it is

Wisdom in Action

counterintuitive to think that we can act in this world while giving it up. Which path should he pursue?

This is such a common misunderstanding that Krishna takes the opportunity to clarify it again, and it will be the second time Krishna rejects the idea of giving up work. Dovetailing our worldly work is safer and more practical than trying to give up the world. Action in karma-yoga is not different from philosophical renunciation in sankhya-yoga. Superficially, they appear different: one seems to be based on detachment and the other on attachment. But they are, in fact, aspects of the same path, with the same goal. In sankhya-yoga, we first focus on giving up our material desires using philosophy, and only then apply ourselves to further spiritual practices. Sankhya-yoga, therefore, remains incomplete if it fails to culminate in practical application. Whereas in karma-yoga we apply ourselves from the outset by devoting our actions and desires to divinity. Karma-yoga combines philosophical analysis (sankhya) and action (karma) to produce 'wise action'.

The typical pattern goes something like this:

Regulation of material desire and dedicating the results of dutiful work to divinity ⟶ helps open our minds and intelligence ⟶ we better understand spiritual knowledge and become more detached ⟶ we are ready for a life of spiritual devotion and love.

Simply giving up material life is not enough to make us happy; we need to live with a positive spiritual connection. There is no meaning to giving up something that does not belong to us in the first place; the wise know to whom everything belongs, so they do not try to give up the world artificially. Their deep renunciation is an internal state free from duality, neither hating nor desiring. They live in this world dedicating everything to divinity, so karmic reactions glide off them as water glides off a lotus leaf. So one who lives in spiritual connection can act in the world without ever being implicated: inaction in action. Such persons are naturally in control of their minds and bodies, which opens the door to deep introspection and thus allows them to comprehend the deeper truth of spiritual equality in all living beings.

We choose to identify exclusively with our mind and body, thereby subjecting ourselves to their pains and pleasures. But by self-control and detachment, we can be more content as observers.

The Self appears to be the master of the body but is neither its proprietor nor its only controller. The Self desires. The indwelling divinity within each of us, the Superself, sanctions these desires to the degree that we deserve, based on our past deeds. And material nature carries out what is desired *and* deserved. The Self, like a passenger in a car, has no *independent* power to act beyond desiring. We need to tell the driver where to go, but that's about it.

Krishna reminds Arjuna that neither giving up action nor theoretical spiritual knowledge is sufficient to satisfy the Self. We need to somehow experience the spiritual reality. For this, the wise take shelter in divinity. For them, everything is revealed, as when the sunrise illuminates every detail around us in a way that no artificial light can replicate.

The wise see everything in divinity and divinity in everything and in every living being. This is the basis of their deep sense of equality and inclusion, beyond just theory or any sectarian boundaries. Through contact with spiritual reality, such persons have reached enlightenment and are released from the cycle of birth and death.

They also experience the Self's sameness in quality with divinity, like a sunray to the sun. Think of the sun pouring through the window of a room. We know these sunrays are simultaneously the same as and different from the sun – they are the same in quality but vastly different in quantity.

These wise yogis do not delight in material pleasures because they know such pleasures are temporary. Instead, they enjoy unlimited happiness within. This is a state of deep spiritual connection called samadhi, or brahma-nirvana: self-realisation.

The even more advanced yogi, along with realising the Self, realises the accompanying presence of divinity within. They patiently tolerate any distractions that may arise on their path. They are beyond duty, yet they continue to work for the welfare of all living beings – working not out of duty but instead out of love and compassion.

Some aim for this end through the ashtanga-yoga system, a mechanical means of sense, breath, and mind control. Krishna will explain the ashtanga system in the next chapter.

Krishna concludes this chapter by confirming that anyone who is absorbed in connection with him, and who knows him to be the ultimate proprietor, the goal of sacrifice, benefactor, and friend of all, easily attains the unending peace of connection with him.

This promise offers the seeker assurance and removes any misconceptions about ultimate control and ownership. We can stop trying to exploit the world or control every insignificant detail, knowing that we are meant to simply be custodians. We can work with renewed vigour, knowing that we are part of something greater than ourselves and not participating in a pointless or doomed life. And we can be confident knowing that any sincere attempt to elevate consciousness will bear fruit. In summary, we can be peaceful.

Direct spiritual experience will help us transform, but that needs the dual ingredients of our effort and Krishna's help; the next chapter explains meditation as one method to get that direct experience…

6

Meditation

The Bhagavad Gita is the essential book on yoga. Throughout the discourse, Krishna explains the various forms of yoga, how they are connected, and how they move us towards increasing levels of selfless love. He has thus far emphasised the ease and practicality of buddhi-yoga, which is based primarily on devotion and incorporates selfless work (karma-yoga) and philosophical analysis (sankhya-yoga/jnana-yoga).

Meditation

In the previous chapter, Krishna described the state of samadhi/brahma-nirvana and mentioned ashtanga-yoga as one practice to get there. The eight (ashta) limbs (anga), or progressive stages, of the ashtanga system are yama (proscriptions), niyama (prescriptions), asana (postures), pranayama (breathing), pratyahara (withdrawing senses), dharana (inward contemplation), dhyana (deep meditation), and samadhi (full absorption). We can see from these eight stages that ashtanga-yoga begins with a commitment to an ethical life and emphasises renunciation in order to facilitate meditation. This is a far cry from modern versions almost exclusively dedicated to postures and breath-work.

Krishna begins by reiterating that true renunciation is an internal state, not just an external disengagement from the world. To progress in yoga, we must renounce selfish motivations, and to do that, we must perform selfless work. As Nietzsche said, 'If you cannot be saints of knowledge, at least be its warriors.' So for a beginner in ashtanga-yoga, karma-yoga is still practised. Only those who have reached the penultimate stage (deep meditation) are advised to withdraw from the world. And once the eighth and final stage (full absorption) is reached, the successful yogi once again engages with the world to help uplift it.

The central focus in ashtanga-yoga is to control the mind and then withdraw it inward for meditation. To do this, ashtanga tries to tame the mind with rules, regulations, postures, and breathing exercises. If the mind is controlled, it will be our best friend, allowing us to meditate and thus realise the Self and divinity within. If the mind is uncontrolled, it remains our greatest enemy. The nature of the mind is that it wants to be directed – it will follow either the dictates of the body and senses or the dictates of the Self and divinity. Which would we prefer? One who has conquered the mind rises first beyond the material dualities of happiness and distress, heat and cold, honour and dishonour. The still more advanced yogi regards even friends and enemies, the 'pious' and the 'sinners', all equally.[1]

Ashtanga requires constant absorption of body, mind, and words, so strictly speaking, a yogi should go to a secluded and sacred place to practise. The yogi's practice must include regulated eating and sleep, accompanied by complete sexual abstinence, careful mind control, and eventually freedom from negative desires and possessiveness. The yogi should then, step by step, meditate upon divinity within the heart. From wherever the mind wanders due to its flitting nature, the yogi must draw it back under the control of the Self. This freedom from disturbance allows the yogi to perceive the subtle Brahman. It was always there, but now it can be appreciated. We are flush with overpowering stimuli that, just as in a meal where strong tastes obscure the more subtle flavours, obscure our ability to discern the more subtle spiritual reality.

The blissful experience of self-realisation and connection with divinity gradually empowers the yogi to remain steadfast, like a lamp in a windless place. Without this experience and connection, the yogi will be easily swayed.

The most highly accomplished yogis then realise that the indwelling divinity is identical to Krishna. They now see Krishna in everything and everything in Krishna, never losing sight of Krishna and Krishna never losing sight of the yogi. This is oneness – the oneness of love.[2]

The perfect yogi understands by dint of their own experience that the root cause of happiness is connection with Krishna, and the root cause of distress is separation from him. Such a yogi can be a true friend in helping others attain happiness. Again, this approach to meditation is radically different from more modern versions that typically lean towards just 'emptying' the mind: it takes us from mindfulness to heartfulness.

But Arjuna has a doubt. He says that the ashtanga-yoga Krishna has described seems impractical and unendurable because the mind is restless, turbulent, and even more difficult to control than the wind! Krishna acknowledges this but says it is possible by suitable practice and detachment. This underscores the importance of a regular and determined spiritual practice: to slowly but surely tame the mind. However, if we are unwilling to regulate our lives, it will be like trying to light a fire while pouring water on the wood.

Arjuna wants to be reassured about the path of yoga and so asks what happens if someone tries but fails to reach the goal. Would they get the worst of both worlds: a life of austerity but none of the benefits? Krishna says that the yogi who fails in the early stages still goes on to great comforts in their next life, and they are provided with material benefits and the opportunity to again focus on their spiritual development. The yogi who fails in the latter stages retains their advanced consciousness in their next life, picking up from where they left off to quickly achieve enlightenment.

Krishna concludes this chapter by summarising that a yogi is greater than an ascetic who is not engaged in the pursuit of self-realisation, an empiricist, or a materialist. Krishna tells Arjuna: therefore, in all circumstances, be a yogi. And of all yogis, Krishna says, the one who with great love constantly meditates upon divinity within the heart is intimately united in yoga with Krishna and is the best of all.

An updated summary progression of yoga can now include ashtanga: the first rung of the ladder is regulation of material desire and dedication of the results of dutiful work (karma-yoga) to divinity; this helps open our mind and intelligence, and we progress to understand spiritual knowledge better and become more detached (jnana-yoga); then we may increase our meditation on divinity within the heart by physical and mental processes (ashtanga-yoga); and then we are ready for a life of spiritual devotion and love (bhakti/buddhi-yoga). These are not discrete steps – there is always some mixing of these different approaches – but visualising it like a ladder helps describe the evolving emphasis, moving ever closer to a refined love devoid of selfish desires.

The various types of yoga accommodate every type of practitioner and ultimately aim to connect us with transcendence; having a clear understanding of material reality and our relationship with it will help, and so Krishna explains this in the next chapter…

7

Knowledge and Wisdom

Krishna has now declared the perfection of yoga: being intimately united with him. Knowledge about a person helps build a relationship, so for one seeking to be intimately united with Krishna, it helps to know all about him and his creation. This includes knowledge of the spiritual reality, of the material world, and the source of both – beyond which nothing remains to be known. Such perfection is attained only by the rarest transcendentalists.

Knowledge and Wisdom

Krishna first lists the material ingredients of the phenomenal world, which he describes as his separated energy – 'separated' because it is empowered to act seemingly automatically, keeping Krishna veiled from the materialist. This material energy is simply a transformation of the original non-dual spiritual energy. In order to appear separated from Krishna, that original spiritual energy becomes transformed by the introduction of both time and the three modes. We will return to this in Chapter 14.

The Self, a ray or particle of spiritual energy (Brahman), gets into trouble when it tries to exploit the material energy. But should we persist, we are given material bodies to carry out our attempts at material enjoyment – enjoyment divorced from spiritual connection.

All living beings, Krishna says, are a combination of these two natures: our essence is spiritual and our bodies material. In summary, Krishna is the source of the undifferentiated non-dual spiritual energy, of which the Self is part and parcel, and of which the material energy is a transformation.

Everything rests on Krishna as pearls rest on a thread: he upholds everything yet remains invisible. Krishna lists examples of how Arjuna can still perceive him in the world and always be conscious of his threadlike presence everywhere. This allows for a preliminary and energetic, albeit impersonal, perception of Krishna.

Krishna says he is the taste of water, the light of the sun, the ability in man, the syllable Om, and so on. Krishna is not only the cause of everything but also its active principle (for example, the thirst-quenching potency of water), its seed (the primordial undifferentiated energy from which the universe springs), and its essence (its purpose, that is, to help us reunite with him or to help us separate from him – whichever we wish). Krishna is thus simultaneously both the sum and substance of everything, by way of his energy, yet he remains completely aloof from everything.

The material energy serves as a potent veil to facilitate the Self's independent endeavours for enjoyment, enabling those absorbed in material nature to remain oblivious to his all-pervading presence. Though called *material* energy, consisting of the three modes of material nature, it is in fact divine – being a transformation of Brahman. Krishna will help lift this veil when we sincerely ask him to. Spiritual traditions often encourage us to develop a genuine spiritual longing and to appeal to the divine for 'grace' to descend; Krishna's lifting of the veil is a form of such grace.

Knowledge and Wisdom

Some people choose not to ask Krishna for help or even acknowledge him. They may be too absorbed in material pursuit, lacking self-discipline, under illusion, or simply dismissive of the very idea of a spiritual reality. Others who approach Krishna may do so out of distress, or desire for wealth, or inquisitiveness. Yet others approach Krishna sincerely, seeking spiritual knowledge and advancement. The last is very rare. And even such a rare person may require many lifetimes of cultivating knowledge to truly understand Krishna and thus seek shelter in him.

Some people choose to worship other personalities in place of God, desiring the fulfilment of material desires in place of enlightenment. They do not recognise that the ultimate source of their faith and any benedictions they receive is Krishna. Such worship is transactional, and its fruits, like the personalities worshipped, are temporary.

Krishna says that the less intelligent do not accept the third phase of transcendence, his supreme personality, as real. To them, Krishna remains covered by the first phase, his impersonal, all-pervading energy. Over the course of centuries, many traditions have debated the personhood of God. Krishna's explanation reconciles this false dichotomy: the ultimate reality is both personal *and* impersonal, transcendent *and* immanent.

Krishna knows the past, present, and future. He also knows all living beings, but none know him. We, on the other hand, are under illusion and deluded – misinterpreting the nature of the world we experience and clinging on to our mistaken duality. We view things in oppositional or binary terms – success versus failure, good versus bad, being versus doing, strength versus vulnerability, and so on – which leads to inner conflict. We are even repulsed by things that we were attracted to only moments ago. We all have intimate experience of this, whether it is the food and drink we consume, the relationships we chase, or the hopes we fancy.

However, those on the path to becoming free from the chain of karmic reactions rise above such delusion; their consciousness gets cleared of material influence. The Self begins to shine through. Such individuals can take to devotion with determination, supported by a strength of character and purpose that arises from the mode of goodness, which is required for success.

Those whose consciousness is absorbed in Krishna know things as they are. They understand the true nature of both material and spiritual reality. They know Krishna in his various forms; they know he is the governing principle of the material manifestation, the demigods, and all methods of sacrifice.

Knowing all this, they remember Krishna even at the time of death – this is significant for Arjuna as he stands on the battlefield, the threat of death all around him.

We are like sunrays to the sun – qualitatively the same but quantitatively different – so depending on the sun makes total sense; the next chapter crystallises the concepts mentioned so far…

8

Reaching Transcendence

Krishna used some multifaceted Sanskrit terms at the end of the previous chapter, so Arjuna wants clarification, and Krishna obliges:

- Brahman refers to the indestructible spiritual energy. Recall from Chapter 2 that Brahman is accessed in three broad phases: an all-pervading impersonal energy, the immanent, indwelling divinity within each of us, and the transcendent supreme personality. Recall also from Chapter 2 that the material energy is a transformation of Brahman. In Chapter 7, living beings were described as particles or rays of Brahman. Thus the term can have varying specific meanings according to context. Here it refers to the infinite number of eternal and individual living beings as the energy of the divine, like sparks of fire. Brahman is a nuanced and complex term, so the word param, meaning 'supreme', is sometimes added when referring to divinity.

- Adhi-atma refers to the eternal Self. While the word atma can also refer to the mind and body, the prefix adhi makes the distinction by referring to its essential or presiding principle. This Self is referred to as a 'marginal energy' because it can choose to identify either with material nature ('I am this mind or body') or with the spiritual nature ('I am Brahman').

- Karma refers to our actions and their consequences. More technically, it refers to all the subtle impressions, inclinations, desires, decisions, and actions – and their implications – that lead to the development of and changes to a material body. These can be positive or negative changes, starting first with the mind or subtle body, and followed by a corresponding physical body. The variety of

material bodies we observe is the unlimited variety of individual karma manifesting in particular ways.
- Adhi-bhutam refers to Krishna indirectly as the energetic source whose energy is the material manifestation. Anything 'material' is characterised as that which constantly changes and ultimately perishes – time erodes even mountains. Our first such reference point is our own body. Our bodies constantly change through birth, growth, maintenance, reproduction, decline, and death. As discussed before, the material manifestation is a transformation of Brahman, Krishna's energy, and only *appears* separated from it as it moves through endless cycles of creation and destruction.
- Adhi-daivam also refers to Krishna indirectly and is conceptually conceived as the personification of the cosmos and its most powerful beings (demigods). This imaginary form will be detailed in Chapter 11.
- Adhi-yajna refers to Krishna more directly as the ultimate recipient and sanctifier of all methods of sacrifice. This form is the indwelling presence within the heart, known as Param-atma, the Superself and second phase of divinity.

These terms show how the universe and our human experience can be explained with reference to Krishna, providing a coherent description. At the end of

Chapter 7, Krishna said that those with consciousness absorbed in him can know him at the time of death and thus attain him. Arjuna now asks how this comes to be. Krishna replies that by knowing him in the above ways – as the source of Brahman, the Self, and material nature, and in his conceptual cosmic form, and as his presence within the heart – one can be aware of him all the time, even at the time of death.

Whatever state our consciousness attains by the time of death, that is the state we attain next. It follows that one whose consciousness is absorbed in Krishna at the time of death attains him after death. This requires practice during life; you cannot just fake it at the very last moment! If we cannot control our minds when we are in good health, it is going to be a whole lot harder at the time of death. Hence Krishna asks Arjuna to carry out his duties with mind and intellect fixed on him. The mind is materially distracted, so what should come naturally for a spiritual being – meditating on the Self and Krishna – has at first to be forced. But this changes with practice.

We might start by meditating upon certain features of divinity, such as the one who knows everything, as the oldest, as bigger than the cosmos and smaller than the atom, as the maintainer of all, as transcendent, as one with inconceivable beauty, and as more radiant than the sun.

Krishna takes the opportunity to explain a technical process of meditation, sat-chakra-yoga, where one chants Om (Krishna's impersonal sound representation as explained in Chapter 7), practises strict celibacy, withdraws the senses, fixes the mind on the heart space, and then moves the prana (life air) to the chakra at the top of the head.

Having explained various types of yoga practitioners, who can attain different elevated destinations according to their motivations and desires, Krishna now reconfirms the state of those who remember him continuously, free from all material desire. For them, Krishna says, he is easy to attain. This path is made easy because Krishna reciprocates perfectly our desires; Krishna himself constantly thinks of a yogi who constantly thinks of Krishna. And having attained him, the highest perfection, these devotees never return to this temporary world.

From the highest plane in this material world down to the lowest, all are places where misery exists due to repeated birth and death. The universe itself is destroyed and recreated, ad infinitum. Even Brahma, the universal engineer and its highest life form (not to be confused with Brahman), is destined to die. His lifespan is equal to the life of the universe.[1] The duration of Brahma's day is a thousand ages – and his night is the same again. Each age is a full cycle of four epochs of time.[2] At the beginning of Brahma's day, all living beings become manifest from an unmanifest state of primordial energy. And at the end of his day, the living beings are merged into the unmanifest state again.[3] This happens again and again throughout the life of the universe. All this is to help us understand that death awaits us all no matter how great we may become in the material world.

Yet there is another place which is not perishable. The Vedic scriptures describe that abode as the supreme destination, transcendental and infallible. This is Krishna's eternal home and the eternal destination for all those who attain him through loving devotion. Krishna pervades the spiritual world with his spiritual energy, just as he pervades the material world with his separated, or material, energy.

But what about yogis who do *not* desire unalloyed devotion? All forms of yoga except unalloyed devotion carry risks because, instead of relying on Krishna, they rely on the stringent technical success of their yoga practice. This includes even optimising the time of one's death to help determine our next destination. This is in keeping with Krishna's undertaking that he will reciprocate our desires: if we don't want to rely on him, he will let us continue relying on ourselves. Refusing Krishna's offer is simply self-defeating.

Krishna concludes that while unalloyed devotees know about the various technicalities of yoga, they are never distracted because they trust and depend on him. Such devotees easily attain all the benefits of scriptural study, austerity, charity, duty, and so on, and reach the supreme destination. At the end of Chapters 6 and 7, Krishna concluded that the devotee was the topmost of all yogis – this chapter explains why.

Whether material or spiritual, we are the architects of our destiny and Krishna facilitates our choices, always hoping that we choose love; the next chapter spotlights the secret of selfless love…

9

The Great Secret

Krishna will recap some of the themes of Chapters 7 and 8. He now explains untainted devotional love, free even from desire for knowledge and liberation. Chapters 2 to 6 have focused on knowledge of the Self and liberation, but it is not enough to know that the Self is different from the material body or that it does not perish. This is necessary but not sufficient; it lacks positive information. Chapters 7 and 8 have more explicitly focused on positive knowledge about divinity so that we can better understand how to relate to it. Chapter 9 will focus on pure, or unalloyed, devotion – the nature and activities of one in perfect harmony with the divine. So special is this that just a sincere *desire* for unalloyed devotion leads to liberation. Krishna has referred to these progressive stages of knowledge as confidential, more confidential, and now the most confidential.

Krishna calls this last stage the 'king of knowledge' because it should rule over all other types. This is because unalloyed devotion gives direct perception of our spiritual Self and thus is the very essence of religion – it is based on experience and not just theoretical faith. Once experienced, this will uplift Arjuna's consciousness and revive him from his deflated state. This path of unalloyed devotion is exalted because any progress made is never lost and because it is joyfully performed.

Krishna speaks again about how he pervades everything and yet remains invisible; to 'see' him requires eyes of love. He is the very source of everything. His energy is diffused throughout the cosmos as his representation. He is the creator, maintainer, and destroyer of the material manifestation, yet he does not touch it directly because, under obligation to his will, all this happens automatically by the forces of nature. Similarly, living beings appear to act as if independent but are, in fact, totally dependent on him. By his mere intention, something becomes a reality. Such descriptions of inconceivable potency stimulate awe and wonder, thus prompting enquiry about the nature of reality.

Yet, Krishna says, fools deride him when he chooses to descend in a humanlike form because they don't understand his transcendental reality. Their misunderstanding is something like a group of prisoners who think the prison warden is one of them just because the warden is also inside the prison. Such persons become attached to their misconceptions and choose to remain under illusion. Those great persons who have moved beyond illusion and delusion, mahatmas, are deeply engaged in a relationship with the divine through various types of loving service. And there are still others (in addition to the four types of seekers mentioned in Chapter 7 who approach Krishna directly) who, by ritual or study, approach divinity, but they do so *indirectly*: some are materialists or pantheists who worship the cosmos as God, others worship a fictional form or a demigod, and some even think of themselves as God.

But it is Krishna who is the ultimate source, ingredient, means, and goal of everything. Krishna again gives examples of how we can see him everywhere and in everything. Both matter and spirit are in him;

thus for the self-realised, there is no difference between matter and spirit because they perceive Krishna's presence everywhere.

The religious who still seek sensory enjoyment can have their desires fulfilled, but after their temporary heavenly enjoyment, they continue their journey in the cycle of birth and death. We all attain a destination corresponding to our practice and object of worship. And Krishna lovingly devotes himself to those on the path of loving unalloyed devotion; this is reciprocation, not favouritism.

Even the smallest devotional acts are full of potency to elevate our desires. Krishna says that if one simply offers him just some water, a leaf, a flower, or some fruit, if it is offered with love, he will accept it. It all belongs to him anyway, but he relishes the exchange of love, like a parent relishes a gift from their young child.

We can continue doing our everyday things, but now as an offering to him: every time we eat, or try to help someone, or while working, instead of just going through the motions, we can instead consciously try to see the bigger picture and act with the intention to serve. We don't have to repress our nature or change our lives before we can dedicate our activities to divinity – it is a matter of consciousness. We can use this principle to raise our consciousness throughout the day by taking a moment to reflect and consider how we might dedicate our actions to divinity. In the beginning, we may simply act and our minds may wander, but gradually our minds will cooperate to make our dedications complete. And tethered to transcendence, we will gradually become free from karmic reactions and proceed to higher levels of connection.

Krishna restates that he, like the rain, is impartial and equal to all; he respects our free will and reciprocates our approach. The devotee reaches out to Krishna with love, and so Krishna responds.

If a devotee unintentionally slips on the path of loving devotion, Krishna says that he helps them from within. There is no need for separate ritualistic atonement; loving devotion is sufficient to reinstate them on the path. Anyone and everyone can attain perfection simply by approaching Krishna with love – no exclusivism, no barriers to entry.

Krishna concludes by telling Arjuna to always think of him and be fully absorbed in him, promising that Arjuna will thus surely come to him. This last verse of Chapter 9 appears exactly in the middle of the Bhagavad Gita and will be almost identically repeated near the end (Chapter 18, text 65). It represents the essence of Krishna's message – his clarion call to us all to join him in a relationship of love...one where we can be whole, joyful, and fearless.

All you need is love, and Krishna is its reservoir and repose; the next chapter reveals how we can take the first step towards such love…

10

The Essence Within

Krishna has delivered the essence of his message: it is a call to all living beings to be engaged in a loving relationship with him. Krishna will continue that theme in this chapter with what many consider a four-verse summary of the whole text. Over the previous three chapters, Krishna made references to his energies. Prompted by Arjuna, he will now elaborate with specific examples. The notion that 'God is great' is common, but knowing *how* great he is stimulates our gratitude and induces us to seek his shelter.

Since Krishna is the origin of everyone, we need him to explain his own nature for us to be able to know him. Such revelation destroys our ignorance at its root. The seeker who understands Krishna to be the unborn and beginningless knows things as they are. One who is thus convinced of Krishna's magnificence naturally engages in unalloyed devotion.

Krishna now delivers his four central verses:

I am the source of everything. From me, everything is set into motion. The wise who know this well offer their love to me with all their hearts.

Their thoughts dwell in me, their lives are fully devoted to my service. They derive great satisfaction and bliss from always enlightening one another and conversing about me.

To those who are devoted to me with love, I give the understanding by which they come to me.

Out of special compassion for them, I, dwelling in their hearts, dispel with the illuminating lamp of knowledge the darkness born of ignorance.

The Essence Within

These verses give us a glimpse into the relationship between Krishna and his devotees. These devotees learn about him by conversing about him, but also by direct revelation in the heart. This direct revelation is 'the understanding by which they can come to me'. Acting on this understanding is what Krishna calls buddhi-yoga. This is a term he has used since Chapter 2, but we now see its fuller meaning. This is not simply 'intelligence', as some might assume from the word 'buddhi'. The term is synonymous with bhakti-yoga, or the yoga of loving devotion; it is the expression of supreme intelligence. These verses also explain how Krishna reciprocates with loving devotees; he gives them understanding and destroys their ignorance. This is Krishna's special favour: he enlightens from within, providing the understanding one needs to reach him. While doing so, he fulfils all the spiritual and material needs of the devotee. When Krishna takes charge in these ways, the devotee becomes completely free from all lesser endeavours. Devotion is compared to a seed, with devotional expressions acting as the waters that nurture the seed, allowing it to grow into a plant that ultimately bears the fruit of divine love.

Arjuna now speaks for the first time since the very beginning of Chapter 8. He is free from doubt and wholeheartedly accepts what Krishna has explained. Krishna has related how he reveals himself to those absorbed in the yoga of loving devotion. Krishna has also given examples of how his energy pervades the world and how anyone can think of him in this way. For the benefit of all humankind, Arjuna is keen for Krishna to explain this further, and so he asks: how can someone who has no love for Krishna also think of him constantly? Krishna agrees to answer. But he can give only an indication since there is no end to the representations of his boundless power. He is unfathomable, yet he desires to become available to everyone.

Krishna indicates how we can see him represented by the supreme embodiments of any given category. Here are some examples he provides: among sounds he is Om; of sacrifices he is the chanting of divine names; among immovable things, the Himalayas; among men, the monarch; of all subduers he is death; among purifiers, the wind; of knowledge he is knowledge of the Self; of those professing theories he is the theorem; of feminine attributes he is fame, beauty, speech, remembrance, intelligence, constancy, and forbearance; among those who seek victory he is moral conduct; he is the silence of secrets; the wisdom of the wise…

Wherever we see great potency, beauty, or any other excellence, we should understand that it springs from but a spark of Krishna's splendour. With just a single aspect of himself, he pervades the entire universe. He is the beginning and end of all energy – the very substrate of everything.

We each have a relationship with Krishna – we develop that relationship by our thoughts, words, and acts, and incredibly, Krishna reciprocates in kind; the next chapter illustrates our dependence on Krishna…

11

Everything, Everywhere, All at Once

Arjuna says that his illusion has been dispelled. He has heard dozens of examples of how Krishna pervades the universe with unlimited powers, but now he wishes to see how Krishna does this. This unlimited cosmic form is conceptual, unlike the transcendent form standing before Arjuna, but he wants to see it anyway. Krishna complies and empowers Arjuna to conceive it.

Everything, Everywhere, All at Once

Instantly, Arjuna can see whatever he desires: past, present, and future, all in one place. Arjuna sees this form as a display of terrific power, effulgent like thousands of rising suns. He sees countless faces and people in that endless form. This awe-inspiring vision shatters Arjuna's natural friendly feelings towards Krishna, and he offers prayers with reverence and wonder. He describes this form as immeasurable, yet he tries to describe the immeasurable.

Arjuna also perceives many terrifying features in this form, and his mood changes from wonder to fear. He sees the destruction of the armies before him, rushing like moths to a fire. He sees this effulgent form covering the entire universe with scorching rays. Arjuna is shaken and asks what the mission of this devastating form is. This cosmic form replies, 'Now I am become Time, the destroyer of worlds,' words that centuries later J. Robert Oppenheimer echoes upon witnessing the first nuclear explosion. Krishna refers here to Time as the great destroyer, the cause of inevitable death. All these soldiers gathered on the battlefield were sure to die; Arjuna could be but an instrument.

Arjuna offers prayers, eulogising Krishna as the foundation and resting place of everything and the end of all knowledge – the known and the knowable. Witnessing all this makes Arjuna seek forgiveness for his past overfamiliarity with Krishna. But there is nothing to forgive: we can each relate to Krishna how we wish. Arjuna's natural relationship with Krishna was that of a close friend, making his intimacy not only faultless but also desirable.

Now he asks Krishna to reveal his four-armed form as the Lord of Lords. The four-armed form is referred to in the Vedic texts and is known as Vishnu, Narayana, and so forth. Krishna complies and then assumes his most beautiful two-armed form. Arjuna says that his mind is now calmed once again, seeing this humanlike form. The form of divinity cannot be grasped by austerity, study, or piety – it can only be seen when Krishna chooses to reveal himself and through the eyes of love.

The chapter ends with a verse that reiterates Krishna's essential message: one who engages in unalloyed loving service – free from distraction and selfish desire – who works for Krishna, makes him the supreme goal of life, and is friendly to all living beings, attains Krishna.

Arjuna recognises Krishna's incredible power and realises that his victory on the battlefield is totally dependent on him; he is inspired to know about this in more detail…

12

The Path of Love

Arjuna wants to go deeper. He has heard Krishna speak about the three phases of ultimate reality as ways in which we can connect with transcendence: the impersonal, all-pervading energy, the indwelling divinity within, and the transcendent person. Since Krishna has endorsed them all, Arjuna asks a pointed question: which seeker is most ideally situated in yoga – one engaged in loving service through a personal relationship or one who approaches the impersonal energy? Krishna has already delineated his opinion more than once, but Arjuna wants to leave no room for doubt.

Krishna answers unequivocally: those who fix their minds on him and always worship him are the ideal yogis. He adds that those who diligently approach the impersonal energy do eventually make gradual progress, but it is a more difficult path. This is because the mind and senses constantly demand engagement, and on the impersonal path, there are no spiritual activities to act as positive replacements for material activities. Nor is there anything we can meditate upon, since the impersonal goal is formless and thus inconceivable. As soon as we try to focus on it, the mind naturally imposes form or image upon it. Even abstract emotions or concepts are quickly translated into mental images of their expression or experience. So the practitioner aiming for the impersonal is left with only a few options for spiritual practice, such as philosophical speculation and attempts to empty the mind. Also, the risk of relapse continues with the impersonal path, whereas on the path of devotion, as Krishna has already said, there is never any loss or diminution. Krishna says that for the devoted he becomes the swift deliverer from the cycle of birth and death. Remember, this is reciprocation, not favouritism. A natural consequence of the impersonal is that there is no personality – so no relationship nor intervention.

Krishna repeats the order of priorities for the yogi:

1. The ideal is to fix one's mind and intellect on Krishna with love and without deviation.
2. If we lack the spontaneous spiritual attraction to Krishna to do that, following the rules and regulations of devotion can gradually settle our minds and cultivate our dormant desire to attain Krishna.
3. If our intelligence is not strong enough to convince us to engage in regulated devotion, we can contribute our time and resources to Krishna's cause. The jaundiced tongue thinks even sugar is bitter! Similarly, our diseased minds may struggle to appreciate the joy of an internal state of devotion. So if we struggle to settle the mind, we can start by just engaging the body in devotional activities.
4. If even that is not possible, we can try to meditate on the divine presence within our hearts, as described in ashtanga-yoga.
5. If we are not ready for this, we can nurture knowledge of the impersonal, all-pervading energy, Brahman, through philosophical analysis.
6. Finally, if none of the above is possible, we can at least contribute to any pious material cause so that

one day, hopefully, this piety can be transformed into spirituality.

Krishna here places karma-yoga (point three) above dhyana-yoga and jnana-yoga (points four and five respectively), which is different from how the yoga hierarchy is usually presented. Krishna does this for several reasons: first, because he is referring to the higher levels of karma-yoga (recall that karma-yoga is an umbrella term as per Chapter 3); second, because karma-yoga is most accessible; and third, because dhyana here refers to theoretical awareness (he is speaking of the beginner rather than the expert) and not realised awareness.

Krishna then lists thirty-five qualities that make a yogi very dear to him, such as equanimity, freedom from envy, tolerance, and not disturbing anyone or putting anyone in difficulty. Such a person is firm in their determination and knowledge, and nothing can impede their progress. And of those very dear yogis, those who wholeheartedly offer their love to him with faith and devotion are the most dearly loved by him.

In response to Arjuna's question, this chapter consistently and emphatically emphasises the superlative nature of loving devotion and that of the seeker on this path.

Wherever we are at, we can make progress on the ideal and easiest path of love; having clarified beyond all doubt the superlative position of loving devotion, Krishna will now provide theoretical and practical knowledge to help us towards that goal…

13

What's What

Krishna has left no room for misunderstanding: the path of love reigns supreme. Arjuna again asks Krishna, as he did in Chapter 8, to clarify some of the concepts and terms he has used:

1. Kshetra (the field of activity) and Kshetra-jna (the knower of the field of activity);
2. Jnana (knowledge) and Jneya (the object of knowledge); and

What's What

3. Prakriti (material nature) and Purusha (the enjoyer).

Kshetra and Kshetra-jna: The Field of Activity and Its Knower

The 'field of activity' refers to the body, with the Self as its knower. We perceive ourselves either as our body or as its occupant – in both cases, we remain its knower. According to our desires and what is due to us, we receive a suitable 'field of activity', an appropriately endowed body to enact our desires. In other words, the body is the field where the seeds of material desires are sown, growing into the tree of material life. We cultivate this field and come to enjoy or suffer the fruits of our actions.

Alongside the Self, Krishna is present as a second 'knower' within all bodies. While our awareness is confined to our own body, Krishna's knowing extends to all bodies; he is the Superself. This concept is depicted in the Upanishads through the image of two birds perched side by side on a tree. One bird – representing us – is engrossed in eating the tree's fruit, unaware of the other bird's presence. The second bird – Krishna – sits quietly, patiently observing, awaiting a moment of recognition from the distracted bird.

Similar is the symbolism of Arjuna and Krishna seated on a chariot: Arjuna is the Self, Krishna the charioteer (depicted sometimes as representing the intelligence), the reins the mind, the horses the senses, the chariot the body, and the battlefield our lives. This metaphor of the chariot, used consistently in the Vedic texts, has, in different variations, made its way through several ancient civilisations.[1]

The 'field of activity' comprises twenty-four components:

- Five elements (earth, water, fire, air, ether);
- Three aspects of the mind, or the 'subtle body' (false ego as our layers of transient identities, intelligence as our power of discernment, and mind as our fluctuating attraction and aversion to all we perceive);
- One primordial energy;
- Five input senses (eyes, ears, nose, tongue, skin);
- Five output senses (voice, arms, legs, anus, urethra); and
- Five objects for the senses (smell, taste, form, touch, sound).

Compared to our modern periodic table based on atomic theory, the five elements appear naive – but they reflect the profound Vedic understanding that a reductive approach will not lead us to understanding what 'substance' finally is.[2] We now know this to be true: quantum theory has superseded atomic theory. The categorisation of atomic elements is not fundamental in that we must then ask what subatomic particles are made from, and then what those are made from, and so on, ad infinitum. This reductive approach, through the very process of analysis, loses the essence of what it seeks to describe, as happens when a person is analysed solely in terms of biochemical processes and elements. The Vedic qualitative approach, on the other hand, gets us closer to the very essence of reality. Physics has arrived at the same conclusion: when you get down to it, there are only qualities or processes – there are no 'things', no irreducible building blocks.

The Vedic categorisation of elements (earth, water, fire, air, ether) represents fundamental patterns in nature. Even mathematical expressions are simplified representations of these deeper patterns. For example, the Fibonacci sequence, often found in nature's spirals like shells and galaxies, is a numerical abstraction of the inherent patterns and structures that reflect the dynamic order of creation. Another reason why the Vedic elements are indeed 'elemental'.

The combination of these twenty-four components rouses our attraction and aversion, producing happiness and distress. The Self's pure, original, and transcendent consciousness is filtered through the twenty-four components of the 'field of activity'. This filtered consciousness, 'chitta' in Sanskrit, detectable as sentience and will, is considered an additional twenty-fifth aspect of the 'field of activity'.

Jnana and Jneya: Knowledge and the Object of Knowledge

Krishna will now explain knowledge and the object of knowledge, but only briefly, referring Arjuna to the Vedanta-sutra and Upanishads for a more detailed explanation. The Upanishads contain many descriptions of meditating on the nature of the Self as a means to understand Brahman, much like studying the qualities of a single drop of ocean water to grasp the nature of the whole ocean.

Real knowledge, Krishna says, is understanding the nature of the body, the Self, the Superself, and how all three are conceptions of Brahman. Material nature is a transformation of Brahman, the Self is a part of Brahman, and the Superself is the source of Brahman. This provides us with the basis for both non-duality *and* duality – oneness *and* difference. We are not forced into philosophical extremes; instead, we can reconcile our intuitive sense of interconnectedness and distinction between ourselves, other living beings, and the universe.

Knowledge, then, is a means to freedom, the means to get out of the 'field of activity' and its tangled web of interactions. Krishna lists twenty items as the means to gain knowledge: humility, detachment, equanimity, a philosophical search for ultimate reality, and so on. Notably, Krishna asserts humility as the beginning of knowledge: learning begins when we accept that we have something to learn. And qualities such as detachment and equanimity keep us fair and open-minded and are therefore indispensable for discovering deeper truths.

The real objects of knowledge are twofold, the Self and Superself, which means that the 'knowers' are the same as the 'knowable'. This important point cuts to the essence of spirituality: it is an internal journey of self-discovery. What we usually take as knowledge is something to be understood 'out there'. Krishna reverses this: 'out there' is the 'field of activity', the body; but real knowledge is 'in here', know thyself.

Krishna restates that only through devotion can we truly understand the science of knowledge and attain him, for real knowledge is nothing but the preliminary stage of loving devotion. We first get to know someone, and then we can love them. This is as true for our real selves as it is for our relationship with divinity.

Prakriti and Purusha: Material Nature and the Enjoyer

Now Krishna explains the last pair of terms that Arjuna has asked about.

Material nature is eternal, constantly cycling through phases of creation, maintenance, and destruction. It is the source of all material causes and effects. The Self is also eternal but, unlike material nature, is changeless. The Self is the so-called enjoyer, ensnared by material nature, pursuing its desires through various 'fields of activity'. In this way, the Self becomes the cause of suffering and enjoyment, choosing to accept these external conditions as its own.

The way out is to learn from a teacher who can help us transform our desire to dominate, enjoy, and exploit this material nature into a desire to serve lovingly.

The Superself is the *true* enjoyer, the witness, and the authoriser. Some perceive the Superself through meditation, some through philosophy, some through their work, and some simply by learning from those with knowledge.

We gain clarity when we understand these truths: the Self desires and material nature enacts according to what the Self desires *and* deserves; despite it pervading the body and being enmeshed within it, the Self is distinct and eternal; all living beings are equal in the most essential and fundamental sense of their spiritual nature. A person who sees from this perspective possesses the vision of eternity.

The chariot analogy lucidly explains the role of the Self, Superself, and material nature; the next chapter gives us a brilliantly practical and foolproof framework for navigating this reality...

14

That Which Binds Us

Krishna wants to teach us the most practical way to disentangle ourselves from the material world. In the previous chapters, Krishna has referred to the Self being enmeshed within the gunas, the 'modes of material nature', goodness, passion, and ignorance. In this chapter, he will explain what these modalities are, how they influence us, and how we can use those very modes to free ourselves from their influence. By understanding the rules of the game, we can learn how to win. Despite our best endeavours to enjoy life limitlessly, we find ourselves restricted – this chapter will explain why that is so.

In the beginning, Brahman transforms into primordial material energy by the introduction of the three 'modes of material nature', which are essentially the very first level of categorisation of material qualities.[1] This primordial energy is dormant potential – it behaves like nothingness. Within this energy, Krishna also places living beings to begin the process of cosmic evolution. To the untrained eye, it may appear that all the different species of life develop from matter; however, Krishna describes himself as the original 'seed-giving father'.

The first evolution of this primordial energy takes place when Time is added to the mix. Time stimulates the interaction of the three dormant modes and the result is material nature, described in the previous chapter as prakriti. The three primordial qualities that pervade every aspect of material nature are now observable: sattva – goodness; rajas – passion; and tamas – ignorance. Krishna will explain the characteristics of each mode in turn.

The mode of goodness is illuminating and frees us from baseness. We can recognise goodness when we feel clarity and serenity. Yet it binds the Self by fostering attachment to happiness and knowledge.

15

An Upside-Down Tree

Krishna presents an analogy: the material world is like an upside-down ashwattha (banyan) tree. This tree symbolises the illusory and impermanent nature of worldly existence. This imagery profoundly impacted Carl Jung, who noted that it 'was of the greatest significance' to him. This analogy aims to help slacken our attachment to the transient material world.

Ashwattha translates as 'that which will not exist tomorrow'. Its roots are upward, and its branches extend down. Where have we experienced an upside-down tree? When we look at the reflection of a tree in a body of water. It looks deceptively similar, but the moment we try to touch it, it escapes us. And we might become so enamoured by the reflection that we forget that the real tree is elsewhere. This is our situation – we are enamoured by the material reflection, but the moment we try to touch it (with its promises of happiness, durability, physicalism, etc.), it disappears. This tree is so complex that nobody can understand its origin or nature conclusively. Situated within the complexities of this incomprehensible tree, we remain trapped and forget any existence outside of it. Jumping from branch to branch, we try to enjoy the different fruits it offers.

The branches are nourished by the three modes of material nature, where different branches represent the different species of life. The twigs are the objects of the senses suited only for a particular type of body and species. Take the tongue and sense of taste; for example, foods like fruits and grain are tailored for humans and their digestive systems, whereas grass is suited to the various species of herbivores and meat for carnivores. Ritualistic religion forms the beautiful leaves that can distract us from the very essence of religion. And like a

An Upside-Down Tree

reflection that rests upon water, this tree rests upon the water of our desires. With the weapon of detachment, sharpened by knowledge and discernment, we can change our desires and sever our relationship with this illusory tree.

Those who are free from false prestige and illusion, who are done with selfish desire, who are not bewildered, know how to take shelter of Krishna and attain his reality.

Krishna again declares that all living beings are his eternal fragmental parts. Spiritual by nature, we struggle with our material surroundings like a fish out of water. Our desires drive the changes in our bodies. As air carries aroma, our subtle body (recall from Chapter 13 that this refers to the three functions of the mind) carries the conception or blueprint of our next body, which is then fulfilled by material nature providing us a physical body to match.

Consciousness is originally transparent, like water, but we overlay it with the various combinations of 'colours' of the three modes of material nature that we choose to associate with. The yogi sees all this through the eyes of knowledge. But distracted by attempts to enjoy, others cannot see things as they are.

Krishna explains his role as the source and potency behind everything that we depend upon for life, such as light, gravity, digestive power, memory, and so on. Even if we are not philosophically inclined, we can cultivate our gratitude and attraction to him by recognising his presence in all those things we are utterly dependent on.

Krishna says that all those in the material world are fallible, whereas all those in the spiritual world are infallible. And he is above them both. Whoever knows him as such knows everything and naturally offers their love to him. This is the most intimate part of the Vedas – and without cultivating the mode of goodness, it is difficult to enter this intimate realm.

Krishna has arranged reality like an upside-down tree, where the myriad bifurcations represent the options open to us; he will now explain the main categories of possible outcomes…

16

Good, Bad, and Ugly

We all have a choice to make. In this chapter and the next, Krishna discusses how the various 'branches' of the ashwattha tree manifest – in other words, how different combinations of the modes of material nature lead to the different types of people we encounter in this world. One very basic way to categorise people is as godly or ungodly. A godly nature leads to liberation, while an ungodly nature leads to material entanglement. One complies with scriptural injunctions, while the other does not care for them.

Krishna lists twenty-six qualities of the godly nature, born of the mode of goodness, including fearlessness, sincerity, peacefulness, compassion, freedom from longing, humility, patience, and tenacity. These qualities can and should be developed. He then lists six qualities of the ungodly nature, born of the modes of passion and ignorance: deceitfulness, excessive pride, arrogance, anger, harshness, and ignorance. Clearly, these should be avoided.

The categorisation into godly and ungodly is archetypal, and so of course what we observe in the world is not as black and white as just godly and ungodly. Nevertheless, like all true archetypes, it provides a penetrating insight into the human condition.

The ungodly believe that the world has no spiritual reality, has no foundation or meaning, nobody in control, and that it is brought about by passionate desire alone. Yet they are fully absorbed in this meaninglessness. They make up their own philosophies and religious principles to serve their selfish purposes and engage in destructive acts. Driven by insatiable lust, they try to enjoy sex and wealth to the utmost limit, thinking, 'This is all there is.' Gratifying their senses is their prime necessity, and so they are always anxious, bound by a network of unlimited desires, illusions, anger, and hedonistic effort. They remain oblivious to the divine within, who is witness to their cruel acts. They consider their endeavours as advancements of civilisation, and many honour them, but the actual result is that people become crueller and more violent towards other living beings. Thus illusioned, they cannot tell that they are headed in the wrong direction. They are enamoured by their own family and assets and constantly obsess about how to improve upon them. They have unreasonable faith in their own ability and have no regard for any other cause beyond themselves. Such a person thinks that they have the right to live by the sacrifice of all others. They see others with more wealth or influence than themselves, yet they believe they are the greatest. Despite the presence of so many good qualities in another, all they see are faults. Unknowingly, they are violent even to their own selves – walking the path of self-destruction. They don't want Krishna, and he allows them to forget him.

Lust, anger, and greed are the three gates that lead to this degraded life. The human form of life is too precious to be wasted on such degradation; therefore, human civilisation is meant to offer opportunities for spiritual elevation. The scriptures are there to guide society towards a godly nature and away from an ungodly life.

Krishna ends by emphasising that Arjuna has an obligation to know what should be done and what should not, and to then act accordingly in this world.

We must choose who we want to be, between the godly and ungodly; in the next chapter Krishna will explain this from the perspective of types of faiths…

17

Types of Faiths

Arjuna knows that the real world is not black and white. He thinks of all those who fall between the outright godly and ungodly that Krishna has just described. In Chapter 4, Krishna said that one engaged in *some* faithful worship is gradually elevated. And in Chapter 16 he said that the ungodly do not care for scripture, but what if someone does both – not abiding by any scripture but still sincerely worshipping at least *something*, but according to their own imagination? Krishna explains that the nature of our faith changes over time, influenced by the three modes of material nature, and this explains the varied types of religious practices and who they attract. The essence of religion, meanwhile, remains beyond even goodness.

Those in goodness worship godly beings, those in passion worship the ungodly for materialistic benefits, and those in ignorance worship ghostly entities. Krishna then illustrates the modalities of food, sacrifices, austerities, and charity as just four examples of corresponding religious practices. This is all to help steer our lives towards goodness.

Those in goodness are attracted to foods which increase lifespan, bodily strength, and mental clarity. These foods are wholesome and pleasing. Foods that are extreme in taste are dear to those in passion, and they ultimately cause distress and disease. Foods dear to those in ignorance are old, tasteless, putrid, harmful, and violent.

Sacrifices done out of a sense of duty by those who desire no reward – on earth or in heaven – are in the mode of goodness. Sacrifice performed for some material benefit or out of pride is in the mode of passion. And sacrifices performed negligently are in ignorance.

Types of Faiths

Austerities can be of the body, speech, and mind. In goodness, the body is engaged in the service of others, in cleanliness, restraint, and non-violence; speech is truthful, pleasing, and beneficial; the mind is satisfied, grave, and controlled. Stoicism helps tame the mind and can increase our capacity to put others first. In passion, austerities are severe and are performed out of egoism. The more we meditate on gratifying our senses, the more the mind becomes dissatisfied. And in ignorance, austerities are torturous and injure oneself or others.

Charity in goodness is again done out of duty and without expectation of return and to an appropriate person to ensure it is well utilised. In passion, it is done with the expectation of some return or grudgingly. In ignorance, it is inappropriately, wastefully, or negligently done.

These generic examples help us understand the modes in greater depth – how they 'look' and 'feel'. Armed with this understanding, we can apply the modes framework to any decision, action, or even thought in any situation. We can pause to ask ourselves questions such as: what is my underlying motive here? How aware am I of the long-term implications? What is making me feel the way that I do right now? Once we have genuinely honest responses, we can check them against the framework and determine which combination of modes we are in right now.

At first it takes some effort as we get used to checking in with ourselves before speaking or acting, but the more we adopt this framework, the more natural it becomes. And very quickly, the easier it feels to be able to regulate our emotions, manage our daily decisions, and predict our broad longer-term outcomes. It gives us agency.

Krishna says that the word *sat* (which means 'real' in the sense of eternal, true, not illusory) indicates the ultimate reality, the Self, a sacrifice performed for divinity, and all things related to such a sacrifice. The Upanishads also use the word *sat* in describing the fundamental nature of Brahman. Therefore, since time immemorial, great sages chanted the syllables Om Tat Sat to raise the quality of intention behind all their sacrifices, austerities, and charity. By doing so, these activities become dedications to divinity and means for spiritual elevation. Else they can simply become distractions on the path.

Religious practices, such as the type of food we eat or type of sacrifice we perform, can also be categorised in terms of the modes and we must choose carefully; Krishna will now consolidate his teachings and bring them into clear focus in the upcoming and final chapter…

18

Arjuna Rises

The armies are still assembled. They have been waiting for almost an hour. Everything hangs in the balance. Everyone is awaiting the outcome of this one conversation, taking place on a single chariot between two people among the many millions gathered. In this final chapter, then, Krishna summarises his teachings and brings us to a resolution.

Chapters 1 to 6 focused on karma-yoga: dutiful action and renunciation. So Arjuna begins this last chapter by first asking Krishna to clarify the difference between renunciation and relinquishment. The first is about stopping worldly endeavours because they are not spiritual. The second is about continuing with worldly endeavours but giving up their results. And what should one do about endeavours like sacrifice, charity, and austerity – should they be considered worldly and thus abandoned?

Krishna explains that any sacrifice, charity, and penance meant for one's own uplift or the uplift of others should never be given up. Such acts should be performed out of duty, without attachment or expectation. Such acts nurture the very essence of religion: transcendental loving service.

Giving up duty out of bewilderment is renunciation in ignorance. Giving it up because it may be difficult is renunciation in passion. The intelligent are neither afraid of disagreeable work nor attached to agreeable work. Thus, they do not suffer 'positive' or 'negative' karma because they act only out of duty. Therefore, true renunciation and true relinquishment can be the same: stopping harmful endeavours while also acting out of duty in necessary or worthy worldly endeavours. The notion of entirely giving up all worldly endeavour is misleading – it is neither desirable nor practical – so we should instead lead an honest life, dedicating our works to a purpose greater than ourselves.

That Which Binds Us

The mode of passion is born of strong desire. It binds us with relentless desires and their pursuits. We sense passion when we notice uncontrollable desires or intense endeavours. This is us relentlessly chasing the dopamine hit and finding ever-reducing levels of satisfaction. It is volatile, and so is always susceptible to falling to ignorance.

The mode of ignorance is born of delusion. It binds us by negligence, sluggishness, and slumber. We recognise ignorance when we feel depressed, confused, and lacking any motivation to work. It is the opposite of goodness, and under its influence, we cannot understand things as they are.

Acting in ways associated with the mode of goodness brings long-lasting positive results. Acting in passion leads to instant gratification followed by misery. Acting in ignorance leads to mistakes and distress.

To the unfamiliar, it may appear simplistic to try to categorise the infinite range of qualitative experience into just three modes. However, these modes, always in flux, combine in infinite ways to produce unlimited varieties, just as the three primary colours combine to produce an infinite variety of colours. The power of the framework lies in its simplicity and universal applicability; it is unlike any other framework in its scope of application. And because it is based on universal archetypes, we can use it to predict, in broad terms, the outcomes of our choices.

We can use this framework like a traffic light system. Goodness is like green; when we detect it, we should feel free to proceed. Passion is like amber; we should ideally wait, but if we must proceed, do so only with great caution. Passion can be a powerful creative force, but it can also quickly become toxic, so 'handle with caution'. Ignorance is like red; nothing good will come from proceeding in this state.

The modes are clearly hierarchical: passion is better than ignorance, and goodness is better than passion. The goal is to transcend them all ultimately – but this must be done stepwise, like climbing a ladder. Or, put another way, they are stepping stones to cross over the ocean of material existence. We will find it practically impossible to jump from ignorance to goodness without going through passion first. If you are a couch potato, you might need to get to the gym regularly before you can commit to regular meditation. Similarly, we will find reaching transcendence from ignorance or passion practically impossible without attaining goodness. Goodness is the gateway to transcendence.

Understanding the influence of the modes helps us perceive that the Self only desires and that the modes of material nature then act to bring about our desired and deserved experiences. This perception loosens the grip of the modes on us as we begin to perceive ourselves as distinct from our body and mind, allowing the modes to recede gradually. This reprieve provides us with a window to experience the joy of spiritual life, even while embodied.

Arjuna asks Krishna to explain the symptoms, behaviour, and spiritual practices of one who has transcended even goodness. Krishna explains that such persons, aware of the workings of the modes of material nature, neither love nor hate – but simply observe and tolerate – the fluctuating symptoms of the modes (illumination, longing, or delusion). They remain aloof, not desiring to enjoy or relinquish the body. They are not affected by honour or dishonour and treat everyone equally. They are not drawn to ordinary activities but engage with unshakeable determination in spiritual activity.

Arjuna asked a similar question in Chapter 2, but this time he also asks how one can transcend the modes. Krishna replies that their spiritual practice helps them rise through the modes and increasingly engage in unalloyed loving service, bhakti-yoga. This path of bhakti-yoga is the means and the goal: it removes any remaining selfish desires and brings them to their original constitutional state of transcendence, Brahman, of which Krishna is the foundation, as the sun is the foundation of sunlight. Once thus reinstated, they can engage unfettered in unalloyed loving service to their beloved.

We can use the modes framework to help release ourselves from the shackles of material life and rise to love; the next chapter provides an analogy to bring the message home…

Impious works that wilfully break social and religious regulations produce harmful results. Pious works, even when materially motivated, deliver beneficial results. However, along with those beneficial results, there still come reactions that draw us once again into the karmic cycle. Imagine someone giving to charity because they want to help but also because they want some recognition. So best of all is work devoid of any self-interest, for this produces no material results – good or bad – and leads to transcendence. While it may appear that such selfless work enacted in the world is indeed producing results, the point is that selfless work does not generate either good or bad karmic implications, either of which would further bind one to this world.

This concludes Krishna's summary of karma-yoga, and he now begins a summary of jnana-yoga, which involves raising our consciousness through philosophical understanding.

Krishna starts by restating the five constituents of action: the physical basis (body), the means (the more subtle senses), the endeavours of the senses, the performer, and the Superself as the ultimate enabler. One who recognises these five constituents as contributing actors, and not just the individual, sees things as they are. We can detect this reality when we notice that no matter how hard we try, we can never control every detail or outcome of an act. This is because we are not the only actors.

We can think of action in two stages. The first stage is subtle: it is the inspiration to act. The components of this are knowledge itself, the object of that knowledge, and the knower. Once an inspiration to act has moved through the stages of thinking, feeling, and on to willing, then it takes the form of physical action. The components of this second stage are the means of action, the action itself, and the doer. Each of these components can be categorised according to the modes of material nature.

- Knowledge in:
    - Goodness recognises the same spiritual quality in every living being.
    - Passion concludes that there are different qualities of spirit according to the body.
    - Ignorance abandons reason and concludes that there is no difference between the body and Self, or that the Self is everything.
- Action in:
    - Goodness is regulated and detached.
    - Passion is intense, selfish, and egoistic.
    - Ignorance is delusional, harmful, and unmindful of the consequences to oneself or others.
- The doer in:
    - Goodness is determined, detached and enthusiastic.

- - Passion is greedy, envious, and moved by joy and sorrow.
  - Ignorance is deceitful, vulgar, stubborn, lethargic, and despondent.
- Intelligence in:
  - Goodness can discern right and wrong, what to do and what not to do.
  - Passion cannot distinguish between right and wrong.
  - Ignorance confidently concludes that right is wrong, and wrong is right.
- Determination in:
  - Goodness is resolute and controls the mind.
  - Passion is fixed on the results to be enjoyed.
  - Ignorance cannot take one beyond sleeping, fear, and lamentation.
- Happiness in:
  - Goodness is derived from self-realisation; it is first bitter (the tough choice) and then like nectar.
  - Passion is derived from sensual pleasures; it is first like nectar (the alluring choice) but then quickly turns poisonous.
  - Ignorance is derived from sleep, laziness, and confusion; it is distressing from beginning to end.

Nothing in the material world is free from these three qualities born of primordial nature.

Krishna then lists how these modes can help us think about ourselves and the types of work that best suit us – like a personality test. If we choose work that we enjoy and that we have a natural aptitude towards, we can more easily turn our work into a form of worship. We are fulfilled and at our best, society benefits, and we make steady and sustainable progress on our spiritual quest. Everybody wins. Krishna lists the four social archetypes, matching the individual's inherent personal qualities with suitable types of work:

- Calmness, restraint, austerity, patience, honesty, knowledge, wisdom, and spirituality are the natural qualities of an educator. They are suited to teaching and advisory roles.
- Heroism, prowess, determination, resourcefulness, courage, generosity, and leadership are the natural qualities of an executive. They are suited to leading and protecting society and ensuring law and order.
- Trade, business, agriculture, and caring for cows are the natural activities of an entrepreneur. Such entrepreneurial persons are suited to creating wealth and managing resources in society.
- Enhancing the life and work of others is the natural activity of employees, typically skilled workers

and artisans. They are suited to the development of aesthetics and ensuring that society is well-functioning.

We are encouraged to work according to our nature. Even though sometimes the duties that arise from such work may be difficult or undervalued, we should not abandon our duty or try replacing it with something that seems easier but does not match our nature. If we do, we repress our nature and will eventually be pulled back towards it. We need to be ourselves. Be honest and authentic. This will bring us satisfaction, fulfilment, and ultimately success. Choosing work that does not suit us, just because it is the easy way out, like all choices in the mode of ignorance, will eventually frustrate and even depress us. Therefore, imperfect but authentic execution of one's own duty is better than perfectly but artificially imitating another's duty: we ought not to pretend to be something we are not.

Every act in this world has some negative aspect, just like smoke accompanies fire, and so we must not give up duty just because we naively consider it tainted in some way – like a warrior trying to shun killing when it is necessary for the protection of society. By dedicating our works to divinity, all defects will be resolved, our minds will be satisfied, and we will be freed from karmic reactions. And from here, we can engage in unalloyed loving service. Clearly, this principle might be misconstrued as a licence for blind following or even abuse of power in the name of religion. Arjuna's thoroughgoing and sincere questions to Krishna exemplify how we, particularly when in doubt, should explore our own duty very carefully and honestly to avoid this pitfall.

This concludes Krishna's summary of jnana-yoga and he now begins a summary of bhakti-yoga: loving service.

Krishna reminds Arjuna that one can understand him only by bhakti, and through bhakti, attain him. Even though engaged in all kinds of worldly activities, a bhakti-yogi is under Krishna's protection and attains him by his grace. Thus Krishna asks Arjuna to act in this way, on his behalf, and depending fully upon him.

If Arjuna represses his warrior nature and refuses to fight – out of ignorance or egoism, thinking that he is the sole actor and determiner of results – his own nature would soon bring him to fight all the same, perhaps in less noble circumstances. Repression simply will not work.

Intimate knowledge is that of the Self and Krishna's all-pervading presence. More intimate knowledge is that of the Superself directing the wanderings of all living beings from within. And the most intimate knowledge of all will be restated imminently...but first...

Arjuna Rises

Krishna asks Arjuna to fully deliberate on his message and then do what he wishes. This is a critical pedagogic principle: Krishna informs, advises, and guides, but he also leaves us to make our own choices. Arjuna, like all of us, must ask questions, clear doubts, discuss, contemplate, and then choose freely. We cannot abdicate our responsibility to choose.

Seeing Arjuna deliberating over all that he has heard, Krishna, impelled by his immeasurable love for Arjuna, restates in two verses the most intimate knowledge of all, the essence of his message: 'Always conscious of me, with love offered to me, act for me. You shall certainly attain me; this I promise you, for you are so dearly loved by me. Relinquish all forms of dharma and simply come to me as your shelter. I shall grant you freedom from all misfortune – do not worry!'

This message, restating the thirty-fourth verse of Chapter 9, stresses the essence of his message, and that of all Vedic literature: in exchange for our offerings of love, Krishna gives us his own self. The Vedic tradition claims this as the last word in morality and religion.

Now Krishna asks if Arjuna has heard the Bhagavad Gita with an attentive mind focused on the essence of his message, and if his confusion has been dispelled. If not, Krishna is prepared to repeat his entire message. Arjuna confirms. His confusion and depression are gone. He rises and takes hold of his mighty bow. He is resolved and ready to perform his duty. The spiritual warrior within all of us awaits the same transformation. And our transformation will transform the world. We simply need to be sincere in our quest and our questions; Krishna will always be there to guide us, from within and without.

The last five verses of the Bhagavad Gita switch back to our narrator, Sanjaya, who utters his final words to King Dhritarashtra. Sanjaya is in bliss having heard the conversation between Krishna and Arjuna. He concludes: 'Where there is Krishna, the Lord of Yoga, and where there is the great archer Arjuna, there will undoubtedly be all fortune, triumph, great power, and morality.'

Dhritarashtra opened Chapter 1 with a veiled question, 'Is there any hope for my sons?' – and here is his answer.

Dear reader, with this, Krishna finished saying what he wanted to say. His heartfelt calling has reverberated over millennia to reach you here today. The rest is up to you.

Acknowledgements

Over the past thirty-odd years, I have benefited from the insights of countless teachers of the Bhagavad Gita. Foremost amongst them is A.C. Bhaktivedana Swami. His *Bhagavad Gita As It Is* first inspired me to study the Gita and remains, to me, its most loyal and insightful version.

Meera Agarwal, Vandna Synghal, Nilamani Gor, Kirti Butkovic, Sundari Harrison provided invaluable feedback and advice on the early drafts.

Rishi Singh helped get this project off the ground.

And the team at Bloomsbury – particularly Paul Vinay Kumar who worked diligently to bring this book to publication.

Notes

Chapter 2. The Way to Peace
1. Brahman is the Sanskrit term for the source and substance of all reality. The material reality is also Brahman but it appears material to us in order to facilitate our desire for independent enjoyment.

Chapter 3. The Art of Work
1. The framework of the three modes of material nature that Krishna refers to is a fundamental pillar of Vedic philosophical literature, and while it will be expanded upon in later chapters of the Bhagavad Gita, Krishna does not delve too deep into its metaphysics, preferring instead to focus on its ethical implications. Readers interested in the metaphysics of the subject are advised to refer to the Sankhya Sutras.

Chapter 6. Meditation
1. This is why yogis at this stage are not advised to become executive leaders, a role that requires discrimination for politics, management, the dispensation of justice, and so on. The yogi's

capacity to navigate dualities changes as they advance further to bhakti-yoga.

2. Patanjali later expressed this same idea in text 3.4 of his famous Yoga-sutra: *kaivalyam svarupa-pratistha va citi-saktir iti* – the bliss of oneness (*kaivalyam*) is experienced within when the potency of the divinity (*chit-shakti*) reveals the Self's constitutional position, after which begins the real life (*svarupena-vyavasthitih*).

Chapter 8. Reaching Transcendence

1. Brahma's 100-year lifespan is approximately 310 trillion years. According to Krishna, time is both cyclical and passes differently across the universe – it is relative, as Einstein figured out. Approximately half of the universal age, that is, 155 trillion years of the 310 trillion years, has passed.
2. The four epochs of time are satya-yuga (the golden age), lasting 1,698,000 years; treta-yuga (the silver age), lasting 1,266,000 years; dvapara-yuga (the copper age), lasting 834,000 years; and kali-yuga (the iron age), lasting 432,000 years. Each age gets progressively worse in terms of human intelligence, virtue, and socioeconomic well-being. We are currently approximately 5,000 years into kali-yuga.
3. Partial universal dissolutions take place at this time, the last having taken place approximately 1.7 billion years ago.

Chapter 13. What's What

1. For example, the *Katha Upanishad*'s use of the chariot metaphor predates Plato's use (427 BCE–347 BCE) by at least several centuries.
2. The Vedic approach to the elements detailed in the Sankhya Sutras has, like the chariot metaphor, made its way through various ancient civilisations in more simplistic and non-scientific terms.

Chapter 14. That Which Binds Us

1. Vedic philosophy does not describe material nature in 'substance' terms; rather, it describes material nature as fundamentally qualitative and is thus more akin to Quantum Field Theory than it is to Atomic Theory.

Selected Bibliography

Bhaktivedanta Swami Prabhupada, A.C., translation and commentary, *Bhagavad-gita As It Is*. 2nd edition. Los Angeles: Bhaktivedanta Book Trust, 1989.

Schweig, Graham, translation, *Bhagavad Gita: The Beloved Lord's Secret Love Song*. New York: HarperCollins, 2010.

Swami, Bhanu, translation, *Sarartha-Varsini-Tika* (a 17th-century commentary on the *Bhagavad Gita* by Visvanath Chakravarti Thakura). 2nd edition. 2003.

Kishor, Vraja, adaptation, *A Simple Gita*. 2nd edition. 2014.

About the Author

Nitesh Gor has been a student of the Bhagavad Gita for over thirty-five years. He is a social entrepreneur, educator, author, and modern-day philosopher recognised for his expertise in Vedic wisdom and its application in leadership, spirituality, and education. Nitesh is the founder of the Avanti schools, which have a unique ethos centred on spiritual insight and a curriculum that includes meditation, yoga, philosophy, and ethics. His previous experience encompasses CEO and director roles across the exploration and investment banking industries. As co-founder and CEO of Dharma Investments, he oversaw the development of the Dharma Indexes, introduced under licence by Dow Jones. His work on spirituality in education and business has inspired various projects, including a retreat centre and farm in the English countryside, a dharma-based endowment fund, and a brand of restaurant and well-being spaces. Nitesh has an MBA from London Business School and an undergraduate degree from the University of London. He was awarded an OBE in the Queen's Birthday Honours List of 2018 for services to education.

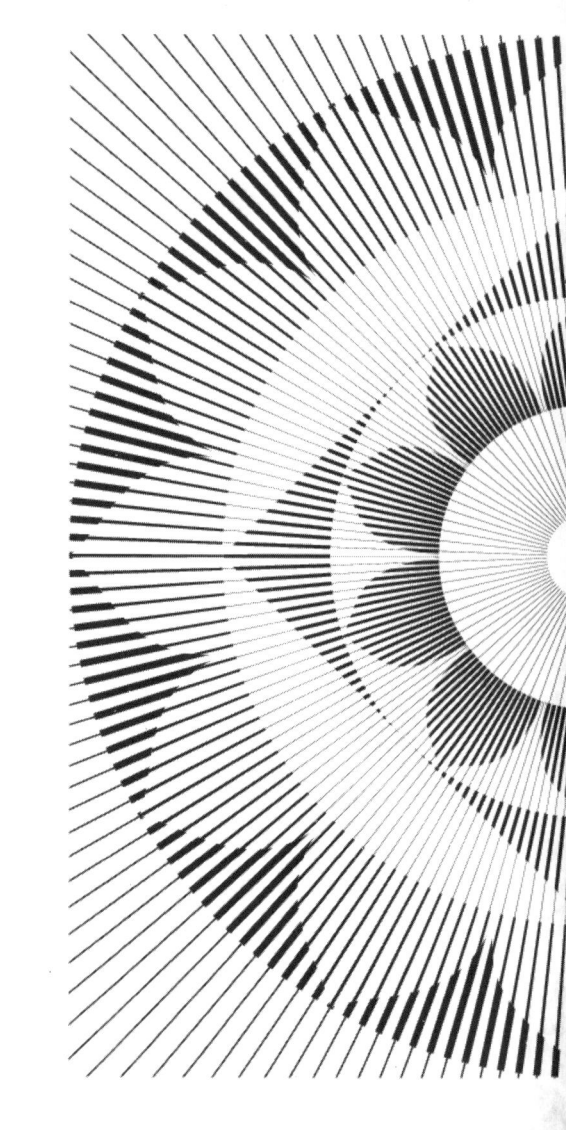